WINE, BEER, AND SPIRITS THE CONCISE GUIDE

A REFERENCE WORK INCLUDING:

*An Explanation of Fermentation and Distillation

*An Examination of French Wines by Major Region, Production Style and Grape

*A Study of California Wines

*An Overview of Italian, German and Australian Wines

*An Explanation of Sherry and Port

*An Examination of Beer Production and Styles

*A look at Spirits and Their Individual Characteristics

WINE, BEER, AND SPIRITS: THE CONCISE GUIDE

By Thomas Owen

**Copacetic Publications
Sarasota, Florida**

Wine, Beer, and Spirits: The Concise Guide

Copyright © 1997 by
Copacetic Publications
1127 Crescent St.
Sarasota, FL 34242

First Edition

All rights reserved. No part of this book may be reproduced in any form or by any means, electronic or mechanical, including photocopying, recording, or by any information storage and retrieval system, without written permission from the publisher.

Library of Congress
Catalog Card Number: 96-85517

ISBN 0-965329-51-8

Printed in the United States of America

TABLE OF CONTENTS

Author's Foreword	07
What is Alcohol?	09
What is Fermentation?	10
Wine in General	11
French Wine	21
Map of French Wines	23
The Loire Valley	24
Champagne	26
Alsace	31
Bordeaux	33
Burgundy	39
The Rhône Valley	46
California Wines	49
Italian Wines	59
German Wines	67
Australian Wines	75
Sherry	79
Port	83

Beer	87
Spirits in General	95
What is Distillation?	96
Whiskey	98
Vodka	108
Gin	109
Rum	111
Tequila	114
Brandy	116
Liqueurs	124
Index	131

Author's Foreword

It is the intention of this book to provide a succinct explanation of the world of alcohol. The subjects of wine, beer and spirits are extensive, requiring of the individual a considerable amount of study and experience to become well-informed. This book will facilitate the reader's learning experience by explaining the *fundamentals* of each of the topics covered. With a proper understanding of these fundamentals, new information will be more quickly and easily understood and more easily retained. This book is intended to be both an interesting study and a portable reference manual. Employees of the restaurant business in particular, as well as anyone else who is responsible for, or interested in the subjects of wine, beer, and spirits will benefit from this *The Concise Guide*.

Thomas Owen

WHAT IS ALCOHOL?

Ethyl alcohol (that which is found in the many varieties of alcoholic beverages) is a colorless liquid having a vaporous odor, and is created as one of the by-products of the process of fermentation on any liquid containing sugar (which may then be further subjected to the process of distillation). Alcohol is a naturally occurring phenomenon that precedes our recorded history, and has accompanied man in almost every society and civilization offering comfort and enjoyment to all but the over-indulgent few. Over the centuries, mankind has developed his understanding and techniques associated with the production of alcoholic beverages but still remains largely beholden to Nature as to the quality and uniqueness of the finished product.

WHAT IS FERMENTATION?

The chemical process whereby sugar, existing in some liquid base, is converted, through the action of yeast, into ethyl alcohol and carbon dioxide:

1 Molecule of Sugar ⟶ **2 Molecules Ethyl Alcohol**
    +Yeast   **2 Molecules Carbon Dioxide**

The liquid base for producing wine is the juice of grapes ("must"), and in beer and preliminary whiskey production it is the malted or cooked grain mash ("wort"). The yeast, carefully selected to impart individual characteristics, begins its work violently at first creating much heat (which must be controlled for maximum efficiency), and continues until all the sugar has been converted to ethyl alcohol and carbon dioxide or until the alcohol level reaches about 15%, which then kills off the yeast.

WINE IN GENERAL

Wine is classed into three major categories: table wine, sparkling wine, and fortified wine. Most fundamentally, **Table Wine** is an alcoholic beverage of varying strength and style created by fermenting the juice of grapes (in stainless steel vats or in oak or other wood barrels). A "dry" wine is one that has had all its sugar converted to alcohol whereas a "sweet" wine has the fermentation process arrested prior to that point (sugar may also be added after fermentation to sweeten wine). **Sparkling Wines** undergo a second fermentation in a closed bottle (or larger closed container) and **Fortified Wines** have brandy added before or after fermentation is complete to alter their taste and alcoholic strength.

There are four fundamental experiences associated with tasting wine:

Color which indicates body or consistency of wine and alcoholic strength,

Aroma, indicating the wine's nuances and subtleties: fruits, flowers, spices, etc.,

Taste, the sensations of sweet, sour, bitter, and salt which are greatly enhanced by the sense of smell, and

Aftertaste, also known as "finish."

Wines can be either ***Dry*** (lacking sugar) or ***Sweet***. White wines can show ***Acid***, a tart freshness which contributes to a wine's aging ability, and can sometimes be over-pronounced, and ***Fruit*** (various distinguishable fruit flavors and aromas). Red wines also demonstrate ***Tannins*** which are organic compounds found mostly in red grape skins, seeds, and stems and in new wood barrels that impart an astringency and bitterness to young wines and body and flavor to a properly aged wine. The proper proportion of ***Alcohol*** is also important to the wine's overall palatability.

WINE IN GENERAL

> *A Note on Decanting:* There are two reasons to decant a wine: First, to clear the wine of sediment. Older wines often require it although not always. A clue is the bottle shape. Bordeaux, California Cabernets, and other wines that may throw sediment come in a bottle that is thinner with sharper, more pronounced shoulders (to catch the sediment) while California Pinot Noirs and French Burgundies, for example, come in a bottle that is wider with more rounded shoulders as they usually require no decanting. Second, decanting allows the wine to breath or mix with air. There is argument about whether this helps or hurts the wine. With some wines it seems to help and with others it doesn't and may actually be detrimental. It depends on the individual wine and on the taste of the specific person or people you're serving.

The activity of producing wine is never an easy job, even with the cooperation of Nature. The factors that most influence the making of wine are geographic location, soil, weather, grape varieties, and wine-making methods (vinification).

GEOGRAPHIC LOCATION: Where the vineyard is located influences what grapes can be grown and how they will develop. In France for example, the northerly Champagne Region produces wines with higher acidity because of a shorter growing season (the grapes have less time to mature and produce sugar) while the more southern area of Sauternes in the Bordeaux Region enjoys a warmer climate and longer growing season, producing many world class, sweet dessert wines.

SOIL: The best soil is that which helps the grapes to maturity steadily: Warm soils (rocky, gravelly) in cooler climates, cool soils (clay, hard earth) in warmer climates. Constant and adequate access to water is important with deeper drainage serving the root system better by providing a more stable environment (and making a sudden downpour at harvest time less likely to swell the grapes with water). The slope of the land is also very important for proper drainage with vineyards on valley floors particularly susceptible to flooding.

> *The insect Phylloxera is another concern for winemakers. A plant louse which feeds on the soft roots of the grapevine, it devastated the vineyards of Europe near the end of the nineteenth century, until it was discovered that American grapevine rootstock was resistant to it. All European vines were subsequently pulled up and grafted onto American rootstock (which did not alter the characteristics of the grapes). A new "biotype B" strain of Phylloxera is now becoming a problem for some areas of California (where American rootstock is proving vulnerable), having wiped out entire vineyards, with more damage likely to follow.*

WEATHER: Access to the sun is essential as it helps to ripen the grape. A southern slope for most areas is ideal as the morning sun warms the soil which then holds the heat as the afternoon sun decreases. Some areas with heavy morning fog benefit more from a western exposure to take advantage of the afternoon sun. Generally, white grapes grow better in cooler climates, while red grapes grow better in warmer climates. Rain is extremely important although not too much rain (watery grapes) or too little rain (dry, under-developed grapes). Spring frost can also be a problem, killing the vine's young shoots and destroying much of that year's harvest, while heavy hail can destroy an entire crop in minutes.

GRAPES: There are literally thousands of grape varieties used by winemakers in the production of wine. Listed below are some of the most frequently encountered:

White Grapes:

**Chardonnay:* It is a versatile grape, able to exhibit differences in vinification methods and local growing conditions. Its wines are dry and full and stand up well to oak. They may be consumed young or, with better examples, aged for many years.

**Riesling:* Competes with Chardonnay for "best white grape." It thrives in cooler climates and its wines can be dry and crisp as in French Alsacean wines or sweet as in German wines, and is also capable of producing sweet dessert wines.

WINE IN GENERAL

Sauvignon Blanc: Produces wines generally lighter and crisper than Chardonnay. Known for its unique "grassy" aroma and flavor.

Sémillon: Produces wines that are rich and full with low acid (although it ages well). Prevalent in Bordeaux Sauternes district because of its susceptibility to *Noble Rot* (the desirable mold *Botrytis Cinerea* which may grow on grapes, and has the effect of concentrating their sugar).

Chenin Blanc: Common to France's Loire Valley and California, its wines may be dry or sweet often demonstrating a pronounced fruitiness.

Gewürztraminer: Its wines are famous for their spicy, fruity aroma and taste. Styles vary from dry to sweet.

Viognier: Comes from France's Rhone Valley. Its wines are generally dry and uniquely perfumed (fruit, orange blossoms, Jasmine).

Red Grapes:

Pinot Noir: A versatile grape which allows for the influence of individual vinification methods and areas of growth. It is thin-skinned and not extremely tannic or darkly-colored.

Cabernet Sauvignon: A thick-skinned grape, making wines that are rich and concentrated and full of tannins which give structure and longevity.

Cabernet Franc: Its wines are lighter in tannin and less intense in color and flavor than Cabernet Sauvignon.

Merlot: Grows well, even in poor weather. Its wines are rounder and softer than Cabernet Sauvignon with less tannins so it may be consumed younger. Can also show less structure and complexity.

Zinfandel: Grown extensively in California this grape makes wine that is dark purple in color, and heavy on fruit flavors and spice.

Syrah: Commonly grown in France's Rhone Valley, its wines are often dark, heavy and concentrated. Australians and South Africans call it Shiraz.

Gamay: Its wines are fresh and fruity with bright acidity and generally little complexity. Grown extensively in Burgundy's Beaujolais district.

Grenache: Hearty grape which grows well in warmer climates (prevalent in the southern Rhone Valley). Its wines are powerful yet often pale red in color. Sometimes used for rosés and blushes.

Sangiovese: Grape used for Italy's Chianti. Its wines tend towards red fruit, crisp acidity, and flowery aromas.

Nebbiolo: Grape used in Italy's Barolo and Barbaresco. It produces dark, heavy, complex wines which can age for years.

VINIFICATION: This refers to the winemaking methods of the individual winemaker and encompasses the hundreds of decisions and tasks from planting, to harvest, to the process of turning juice to wine (including whether there will be oak or stainless steel fermentation, any blending of wines, and if there will be bottle aging); in its finer manifestations it is truly an Art.

> "At the first cup man drinks wine,
> at the second, wine drinks wine,
> at the third, wine drinks man."
> *Oriental Proverb*

FRENCH WINE

Wine-making in France dates back to the sixth or seventh century B.C. It was later that the Romans established what are now the highest quality vineyard areas settling first in the Rhone Valley and Bordeaux, moving into Burgundy in the second century, the Loire Valley in the third, and Champagne in the fourth century. The first vines used came from Italy, Spain, the Alps, and the Rhineland. The descendents of these vines are those growing today because of their continued selection and re-selection for new plantings. French wines continued their development largely unchecked until 1932 when the *Institut National des Appellations d'Origine des Vins et Eaux-de-Vie* (I.N.A.O.) was established.

The I.N.A.O., an official body whose members come from the French Civil Service or the Wine Industry, is responsible for setting the conditions by which a wine may claim its approval.

Appellation d'Origine Contrôlée (A.O.C.) is the highest rating and the guidelines it must follow include: The origin of the wine (accepted areas of growth and production), the grape varieties used, minimum alcohol content, the amount of wine produced per land area (hectare), and viticultural and vinicultural methods used. This rating applies to only better wines and accounts for about 35% of all French wine.

Vins Délimités de Qualité Supérieure (V.D.Q.S.) allows for larger crops and sometimes lower alcohol minimums. It is often a training ground for future A.O.C. wines.

Vins de Pays (country wine) is somewhat more limited than the most common rating

Vins de Table or ordinary table wine accounting for about 25% of all French wine.

Additionally, each region in France has a different I.N.A.O. rating system to further classify the wines it produces and those will be discussed individually. France is comprised of six major winemaking regions: The Loire Valley, Champagne, Alsace, Bordeaux, Burgundy, and The Rhône Valley.

WINES OF FRANCE
By Major Region, District, and Appellation

LOIRE VALLEY
Pouilly Sur Loire
Pouilly Fumé
Sancerre
Vouvray
Saumur
Chinon
Bourgueil
Anjou
Coteaux du Layon
Muscadet

CHAMPAGNE
Non-Vintage
Vintage
Rosé
Blanc de Blancs
Blanc de Noirs
Cuvée de Prestige
Crémant
Coteaux Champenois

ALSACE
Riesling
Gewürztraminer
Pinot Blanc
Tokay Pinot Gris
Crémant d' Alsace

BORDEAUX
Médoc
Haut Médoc
  St-Estèphe
  Pauillac
  St-Julien
  Margaux
  Moulis
  Listrac
Pomerol
Graves
St-Émilion
Sauternes
Premières Côtes-
  de Bordeaux
Côtes de Bourg
Côtes de Blaye
Entre-deux-Mers

BURGUNDY

Côte d' Nuit
Marsannay-la Côte
Fixin
Gevrey-Chambertin
Morey St-Denis
Chambolle-Musigny
Vougeot
Flagey-Echézeaux
Vosne-Romanée
Nuits St-Georges
Côte de Nuits-Villages

Côte d' Beaune
Ladoix-Serrigny
Aloxe-Corton
Pernand-Vergelesses
Savigny-Les-Beaune
Beaune
Chorey-Les-Beaune
Pommard
Volnay
Monthélie
Meursault
Auxey-Duresses
Puligny-Montrachet
Chassagne-Montrachet
St. Aubin
Santenay
Côte de Beaune-Villages

Chablis
Petit Chablis
Chablis
Chablis Premier Cru
Chablis Grand Cru (7)

Côte Chalonnaise
Mercury
Givry
Rully
Montagny
Bourgogne Aligoté
  de Bouzeron

Mâconnais
Mâcon Blanc
Mâcon Supérieur
Mâcon-Villages
St-Véran
Pouilly-Vinzelles
Pouilly-Fuissé

Beaujolais
Beaujolais
Beaujolais Supérieur
Beaujolais-Villages(39)
Beaujolais Cru (10)

RHÔNE
North:
Côte Rôtie
Château Grillet
Condrieu
St-Joseph
Crozes-Hermitage
Hermitage
Cornas
St-Péray
South:
Lirac
Tavel
Châteauneuf-
  du-Pape
Beaumes de Venise
Gigondas
Rasteau
Côtes du Ventoux

> *A Note on French Pronunciation: There are two simple rules to follow when pronouncing French words: Accents are important - if one is shown favor the marked syllable, and if no accent is shown then pronounce each syllable with equal stress (or raise your voice slightly on the final syllable if this is not possible); also, in general do not pronounce the final letter of a French word if it is a consonant.*

THE LOIRE VALLEY

Running along the Loire River for approximately 600 miles in northwest France, it produces quality still and sparkling red, rosé, and white wines. About 75% of its wines are white wines and most are meant to be consumed young with the exception of sweet Vouvrays which may

WINES OF THE LOIRE VALLEY

be aged. The commune *Pouilly Sur Loire* produces dry white wines made from the Chasselas grape with or without the addition of Sauvignon Blanc. It is called *Pouilly Fumé* if it is produced from 100% Sauvignon Blanc grapes and has a somewhat smokier flavor. *Sancerre* offers light, fruity and acidic wines made from 100% Sauvignon Blanc grapes. *Vouvray* is produced from 100% Chenin Blanc grapes and ranges anywhere from dry to sweet. *Saumur* produces white and rosé medium-dry sparkling wines blending a wide variety of grapes and sometimes using the appellation *Crémant de Loire*. The communes *Chinon* and *Bourgueil* use the Cabernet Franc grape and produce wines in the style of *Beaujolais*. The *Anjou* commune is famous for its rosés as well as the vineyard *Savennières* which contains two smaller appellations: *La Roche aux Moines* and *La Coulée de Serrant*. These intensely dry white wines are produced from the Chenin Blanc grape and need up to fifteen years bottle aging. *Côteaux du Layon* makes good sweet white wines from 100% Chenin Blanc grapes with the vineyards *Bonnezeaux* and *Quarts de Chaume* having their own appellations for sweet, rich dessert wines. The commune *Muscadet* makes a bone dry white wine from

100% Muscadet (Melon) grapes. When labeled *Sur Lie* it means the wine was aged with its yeast sediment, and it may have a slight sparkle.

CHAMPAGNE:

It is the northernmost wine-making region of France producing primarily sparkling wines from three grape varieties only: Pinot Noir, Pinot Meunier, and Chardonnay. A Benedictine monk, Dom Pérignon, is said to have been the first to blend wines, and is also attributed with discovering the second fermentation which gives Champagne its "sparkle" (He is said to have commented upon tasting it for the first time: "Oh, come quickly! I'm drinking stars!"). The second fermentation associated with Champagne occurred naturally before the days of careful temperature control because of the area's northerly location. A cold fall would stop fermentation before all the sugar had been converted to alcohol, and with the coming of spring, would restart. All Champagne is a blend of various wines (called a *cuvée*) often from various years so no vineyard name or vintage will be shown. Instead, it is the producer with whom the reputation lies. There are over 130 Champagne houses in France some of the most famous being *Moët & Chandon, Mumm, Perrier-Jouët, Taittinger, and Veuve Cliquot*. In France, the name "Champagne" is protected as meaning only those sparking wines which come from the delimited area of the Champagne Region. In the United States no such protection exists so anyone may use the name "Champagne" on their sparkling wine. All A.O.C. sparkling wines (including Champagne) must be made by the *Méthode Champenoise* which is described below.

The first step is the pressing of the grapes. The first pressing yields the juice from which the highest quality Champagnes will be made, while the second and third pressing yield juice to be used for lessor Champagnes. The next step is fermenting the juice, allowing for the production of ethyl alcohol and carbon dioxide (the carbon dioxide is allowed to dissipate in this first fermentation). Following fermentation, various still wines from the Champagne Region will be blended together with the winemaker deciding the wine of what grapes to blend and in what quantities, as well as from what vineyards and what years of growth. The decisions made here have more to do with the quality of the final product than any other step in the process. Next, the blended wine is put in its permanent bottle and capped after a blend of sugar and yeast (*Liqueur de Tirage*) is added to begin a second fermentation (lower quality sparkling wines not using *Méthode Champenoise* often use large tanks for the second fermentation or simply inject carbon dioxide into the still wine). After the second fermentation is complete the wine is allowed to age with the yeast sediment, sometimes for many years. Eventually the yeast sediment will be removed and this is accomplished through the process of "riddling" or *remuage*, a procedure whereby the bottle is gradually turned and tipped to concentrate the sediment in its neck. Riddling occurs every three days for about six to eight weeks until the bottle is standing straight up on its temporary cap and all the sediment is concentrated. The next step is *dégorgement*, the process of removing the collected yeast sediment from the bottle. The neck of the bottle is dipped into a cold brine solution, freezing the sediment and a small amount of wine. The temporary cap is removed, the bottle is tipped upright, and the frozen plug of wine and sediment bursts out followed by a small amount of foaming wine. After *dégorgement* a small amount of mature wine and high quality sugar is added to replace lost wine and determine the Champagne's final degree of sweetness. The bottle then receives its permanent cork and wire cage and is ready for labeling, shipment, and sale.

The labeling term ***Brut*** refers to a very dry Champagne, ***Extra Dry*** refers to a dry Champagne, ***Sec*** to a slightly sweet Champagne, ***Demi-Sec*** to a distinctly sweet Champagne and ***Doux*** to a very sweet Champagne (these terms refer generally to levels of sweetness although one producer's Brut may be slightly drier or sweeter than another's).

> *Madame Lilly Bollinger on Champagne: "I drink it when I'm happy and when I'm sad. Sometimes I drink it when I'm alone. When I have company I consider it obligatory. I trifle with it if I'm not hungry and drink it when I am. Otherwise I never touch it - unless I'm thirsty."*

The following appellations apply to wines from the Champagne Region:

Non-Vintage refers to a Champagne that is blended from a variety of different years and is aged for a minimum of one and one half years. It is a consistent product and is generally meant to be consumed young.

Vintage refers to Champagne that is blended from a specific year (chosen by the individual producer) and aged for no less that three years, and usually for five (Champagne will not improve in the bottle after purchase although better vintages will keep for some time).

Rosé refers to a blend of white Champagne with still red wine.

Blanc de Blancs indicates a Champagne made from 100% Chardonnay grapes.

Blanc de Noirs refers to a Champagne that is produced from a blend of wine from red grapes only (Pinot Noir and Pinot Meunier), and is sometimes faintly pink.

Cuvée de Prestige indicates the best of a producer (for example, *Moët & Chandon's Dom Pérignon*).

Crémant refers to a half-pressure Champagne.

Coteaux Champenois indicates still white and red wine from the Champagne vineyards.

THE WINES OF ALSACE

ALSACE

Located in the northeast corner of France, running north to south for approximately seventy miles (and between one and two miles wide), it borders Germany and although the region uses many of the same grapes in its wine production as does Germany, it produces wines entirely unlike its German counterparts. Almost all Alsacean wines are white wines and most ferment all existing sugar (and are often vinified in oak), producing very dry white wines which can sometimes have a slight sparkle. Unlike most of the rest of France, the Alsace region produces varietals, that is, wine made from a specific grape. When so labeled it indicates that the wine was made from 100% of the variety named. The four most prevalent grape varieties used by Alsacean wine-makers are Riesling, Gewürztraminer, Pinot Blanc, and Tokay Pinot Gris. Alsacean **Rieslings** tend to be very dry, austere wines. **Gewürztraminers** have a spicy, fruity aroma and flavor. **Pinot Blanc** makes a simple dry, fresh white wine, while **Tokay Pinot Gris** makes dense rich white wines. The region also produces sparkling wines which may use the appellation *Crémant d' Alsace* (all its rosé sparkling wines are made from 100% Pinot Noir grapes).

*Alsace is the basic appellation for the region indicating the wine was made from any of the permitted grapes, crop yield does not exceed the maximum allowed and alcohol content be at least 8.5%.

*Alsace Grand Cru further restricts crop yields, and guarantees a slightly higher alcohol content.

*Alsace Grand Cru (with a vineyard name) is the same as Alsace Grand Cru but indicates also that the grapes came from the vineyard named.

Although there are over 30,000 acres planted in the Alsace region the average plot of land is only three acres. Because of this fact, it is not feasible for most landholders to produce, bottle, and market their own wine, so instead, they sell their grapes to a shipper who does this under his name. Some of the more reliable shippers are *F.E. Trimbach, Hugel & Fils, Domaine Zind-Humbrecht, Léon Beyer, and Dopff "Au Moulin."* All Alsacean wine is bottled in the tall, green Alsacean "flute" bottle and although the wine is sold to shippers, it must be bottled in the region and cannot be shipped in casks.

> *"Wine brings to light the hidden secrets of the soul."*
> Horace

BORDEAUX

Located in the southwest corner of France, it encompasses 54 A.O.C. approved wine areas, with over 9000 different chateaus, covering more than 188,000 acres of land. Its white wines are made primarily with Sémillon and Sauvignon Blanc, while its red wines are a blend of Cabernet Sauvignon, Merlot and Cabernet Franc (and sometimes Petit Verdot and Malbec). The wines of Bordeaux are generally classed into one of three levels: ***Proprietary Wines*** (table wines given a specific name, for example *Mouton Cadet*), ***Regional Wines*** (wines coming from a specific district such as a Sauternes or Graves), and ***Château Wines*** (wines produced from grapes grown on château property and bottled at the château). A *Château* is defined as a vineyard with a house connected, having a specific land area, as well as winemaking and wine storage facilities on the property (other terms used include *domaine, cru, and clos*). With the wines of Bordeaux, vintage or year of production is very important, followed by its classification or ranking, then its age, and finally its area of growth. There are a total of nine winemaking districts in Bordeaux, five major: Médoc, Pomerol, St.-Émilion, Graves, and Sauternes, and four lessor: Premières Côtes de Bordeaux, Côtes de Bourg, Côtes de Blaye, and Entre-deux-Mers.

> *Keep in mind that the word "Claret" is an English word referring to wines similar in style to the red wines of Bordeaux and has no legal meaning in France.*

MÉDOC is the most important area of Bordeaux, and the district which received the famous 1855 Paris Exhibition Classification. Wine industry brokers of the day gathered

THE WINES OF BORDEAUX

together to rank the top wines of the district into one of four classes:

***Grand Crus Classés**, further divided into five quality levels referred to as "growths" and including the top 61 châteaus,

***Grand Crus Bourgeois Exceptionnels**, wine produced in the areas of the *Grand Crus Classés* and bottled at the individual château,

***Grand Crus Bourgeois**, château produced and bottled wine with the additional stipulation that it be vinified in oak, and

***Crus Bourgeois**, château produced and bottled wine.

Of the 61 châteaus to be included in the Grand Cru Classés ranking, the top five or Premiers Crus (also called First Growths) are:

*Château Lafite-Rothschild,
*Château Latour,
*Château Margaux,
*Château Mouton-Rothschild, and
*Château Haut-Brion.

The only change to the 1855 Classification occurred in 1973 when Château Mouton-Rothschild classification was changed from second growth to first growth and, the only château included in the classification not located in

Médoc is Château Haut-Brion of Graves. Although the 1855 Classification is no longer completely accurate (some châteaus no longer exist, while others have increased their holdings) it still remains an important tool for understanding and judging the wines of Médoc.

> *"I had to cook a dinner glorious enough to complement the Lafite. It took four days..."*
> Gael Greene

There are eight appellations in the Médoc area: Médoc, indicating wines from the north, Haut-Médoc, indicating wines from the south and the area where six inner appellations are located: Margaux, Pauillac, St. Julien, St. Estèphe, Moulis and Listrac. *Margaux* has more Grand Crus Classés Châteaus than any of the other six (twenty-one), *Pauillac* has the most First Growths (three) and Fifth Growths (twelve), *St. Julien* is the smallest appellation in the Médoc having no First or Fifth Growths, and *St. Estèphe* having only five ranked Châteaus. *Moulis and Listrac* have no ranked Châteaus.

THE WINES OF BORDEAUX

POMEROL is the smallest of the five major districts of Bordeaux, and has no official classification for its wines. It grows mostly Merlot, and is home to one of the expensive wines of Bordeaux, *Chateau Pétrus*. Made from 95% Merlot grapes, it is an excellent example of the wines generally produced in this area.

ST-ÉMILION produces two-thirds as much wine as all of Médoc, and its wines were classed in 1955 with over seventy Grand Cru Classés, eleven of which are First Growths.

GRAVES gets its name from its gravelly soil and produces both red and white wines (using Sémillon and Sauvignon Blanc in varying amounts for its white wines). It received Classification in 1959 and its wines are grouped into three general categories:

Graves, wine from anywhere in the district,

Graves Supérieures, again, wine from anywhere in the district but with a slightly higher alcohol minimum,

Classified Châteaux, (*Château Olivier* - 65% Sémillon, and *Château Carbonnieux* - 65% Sauvignon Blanc, being two famous classified white wines), and also

Pessac-Léognan, a newer communal appellation which is home to Château Haut-Brion as well as many other excellent châteaus.

SAUTERNES is an area of Bordeaux famous for its sweet dessert wines and is comprised of five villages: *Sauternes, Barsac* (which also has its own appellation), *Bommes, Fargues, and Preignac.* The wines of Sauternes are either regional wines using the general Bordeaux appellations, or Classified Châteaus in three levels:
Grand Premiere Cru, there is only one, Château D'Yquem, the undisputed "King" of the district, ***Premier Cru***, of which there are eleven, and ***Deuxièmes Cru*** or Second Growth (twelve).
The wines of Sauternes are produced from mostly Sémillon with the addition of some Sauvignon Blanc, and in a good year, the Sémillon grapes will be affected by *Botrytis Cinerea* or *Noble Rot* (a desirable mold which grows on the grapes, causing their skin to become porous, allowing water to evaporate and sugar to concentrate). Some years this simply won't happen so the vintage or year of growth is very important for wines from this district. Virtually all of its wines are the sweet dessert variety (achieved by stopping fermentation prior to the exhaustion of all the

sugar) and its better examples can handle age well (up to fifty years).

BURGUNDY

Located in central eastern France, Burgundy is comprised of five major wine producing districts: The Côte d'Or (which is further divided into the Côte d'Nuit and the Côte d'Beaune), Chablis, Côte Chalonnaise, Mâconnais, and Beaujolais. All red wines from the Burgundy Region are made from 100% Pinot Noir grapes, with the exception of Beaujolais which is made from 100% Gamay grapes. Most Burgundian white wines are made from 100% Chardonnay grapes, although the Aligoté and Pinot Blanc grapes are occasionally used in some white wine production. There are many vineyards in the Burgundy Region with the largest being 126 acres and the smallest only two acres. Most of these vineyards are held by many owners (in some cases, over sixty), and each individual owner produces and bottles his own wine. It is called "Estate Bottled" when the grapes are grown, and the wine vinified and bottled by a single producer, and has not been blended with any other wine (the producer's name will then appear on the bottle). Burgundy wine can also be purchased by shippers (*négociants*) who may blend different wines from a specific district together, indicating on the label that this wine is their offering of that individual district. Many of the

> *When reading a Burgundy wine label, if it indicates only a village name then it is a simple **Village Wine** from anywhere in the region and may be blended. If it lists both the village name and a vineyard name it is a **Premier Cru** wine, or one that is produced by a specific winemaker and vineyard. If only a vineyard name is shown, it is a **Grand Cru** wine or the finest single-producer wines available.*

finer Burgundies own their greatness to the outstanding soil in the area and the vineyard's location on one of the many southern slopes, offering good drainage for the vine's root system and adequate sun. Because of the area's unpredictable weather, vintages are very important to finding a good Burgundy wine, with 1985 generally considered to be the best vintage year since 1969.

The ***CÔTE D'OR*** (Golden Slope) is a narrow section of land (about one half mile wide) that runs north to south for approximately thirty miles, through a series of southeastern facing slopes. Wines are classed as:

*****Burgundy or "Bourgogne,"*** a generic appellation that is available for the entire region,

*****Village*** wines,

*****Premier Cru*** wines of which there are hundreds, and

*****Grand Cru*** wines, with Grand Cru representing the best of the area.

In the late 1800's some of the villages began to include its most famous vineyard's name along with the village name, creating many of the hyphenated names found here.

CÔTE de NUIT is the northernmost section of the Côte d'Or and produces mostly red wines. Its major appellations are: ***Marsannay-la-Côte, Fixin, Gevrey-Chambertin, Morey St-Denis, Chambolle-Musigny, Vougeot, Flagey-Echézeaux, Vosne-Romanée*** (where the world famous *Romanée-Conti* and *La Tâche* vineyards are located), ***Nuits St-Georges,*** and ***Côte d' Nuit-Villages*** (a general appellation for five others:

Fixin, which also has its own appellation, *Brochon, Prissey, Comblanchien, and Corgoloin*.)

CÔTE de BEAUNE comprises the southern half of the Côte d'Or and produces both white and red wines. Its major appellations are: **Ladoix-Serrigny, Aloxe-Corton** (*Corton* being the only red Grand Cru in the Côte d'Beaune district), **Pernand-Vergelesses, Savigny-Les-Beaune, Beaune, Chorey-Les-Beaune, Pommard, Volnay, Monthélie, Meursault** (which produces excellent white wines from 100% Chardonnay grapes), **Auxey-Duresses, Puligny-Montrachet and Chassagne-Montrachet** (both which also produce excellent white wines from 100% Chardonnay grapes), **St-Aubin, Santenay,** and **Côte d' Beaune-Villages** (a fallback appellation for almost the entire district's red wines and used by *Cheilly-Les- Maranges, Sampigny-Les-Maranges, Dezize-Les-Maranges, and St-Romain*).

"Montrachet should be drunk kneeling, with one's head bared."
Alexandre Dumas

THE WINES OF BURGUNDY

CHABLIS is the northern most wine producing district in Burgundy, offering dry, "flinty" tasting wines produced from 100% Chardonnay grapes and are quite pale in color, with its finer examples needing some age to mature. There are more than 4000 acres planted although only 245 acres are reserved for the seven Grand Cru vineyards. Chablis is classed in four different categories:
****Petit Chablis***, the most common, although it is rarely exported to the United States,
****Chablis***, from anywhere in the district,
****Chablis Premier Cru***, from a particular vineyard, unless none is named and then it is a blend from any of twenty-nine premier cru vineyards, and
****Chablis Grand Cru***, the seven vineyards entitled to this, the highest appellation, are *Les Clos, Vaudésir, Valmur, Blanchots, Les Preuses, Grenouilles, and Bougros.*

CÔTE CHÂLONNAISE, located just south of the Côte d'Beaune, is home to only five villages, each having its own appellation. ***Mercurey*** and ***Givry*** produce mostly red wines from the Pinot Noir grape, ***Rully*** and ***Montagny*** produce mostly white wines from the Chardonnay and Pinot Blanc grapes, and the village of Bouzeron produces a wine from the Aligoté grape, and uses the appellation **Bourgogne Aligoté de Bouzeron**.

MÂCONNAIS is the southernmost white wine producing area of Burgundy located just below the Côte Chalonnaise. It produces mostly white wines from Chardonnay and Pinot Blanc grapes, its most familiar being Pouilly Fuissé.

*Mâcon Blanc is the basic appellation for the district, requiring a minimum alcohol content of 10%.

*Mâcon Supérieur is the same as above with a minimum of 11% alcohol.

*Mâcon-Villages indicates a wine from any of forty-three vineyards in the east of the district (the name of which will be shown on the label) and a minimum of 11% alcohol.

*St-Véran is the same as Mâcon Villages but refers instead to eight of the southernmost villages, and is made from 100% Chardonnay grapes.

*Pouilly-Vinzelles (100% Chardonnay) indicates that the wine is from one of two village areas: Pouilly Vinzelles or Pouilly Loché and must have at least 12% alcohol (or 11% if no village name is shown).

THE WINES OF BURGUNDY

Pouilly-Fuissé* (also 100% Chardonnay) refers to wines from the area around the villages Pouilly and Fuissé and is the same as to alcohol content as the appellation Pouilly Vinzelles.

BEAUJOLAIS is the southernmost wine producing district of Burgundy and is famous for its light, fruity, uncomplicated red wines. Produced from 100% Gamay grapes, it is meant to be drunk young, particularly ***Beaujolais Noveau***, a wine that is produced and sold in a matter of weeks every fall, with its release date always being the third Thursday in November. It is a very light, fruity and enjoyable wine acting also to indicate to the consumer the quality of the vintage, and the winemaker's production style. With over 55,000 acres planted, and over 2,500 producers of Beaujolais wine there is plenty for everyone. The appellations for the district are as follows:

****Beaujolais,*** the basic wine from anywhere in the district with a minimum alcohol content of 9%,

****Beaujolais Supérieur,*** the same as above but with a minimum alcohol content of 10%,

****Beaujolais-Villages***, usually a blend of any of 39 villages with a minimum alcohol content of 10%, and

Beaujolais Cru, (10% alcohol minimum) of which there are ten: *Moulin-à-Vent, Fleurie, Brouilly, Morgon, Côte de Brouilly, Chiroubles, St-Amour, Juliénas, Chénas, and Régnié.* These "Cru" wines are often more complex and longer lasting, and usually do not show the name Beaujolais on the label so as to avoid being confused with basic Beaujolais.

> *"Ferment the Gamay from my lands in a large vat. Add the laughter of a girl, the spring scents of a garden and a good dose of the spirit of Montmartre."*
> Author Unknown

RHÔNE VALLEY

Located in southeast France below the Region of Burgundy, the Rhône Valley produces white, rosé, and sparkling wines but is most dedicated to its red wines (accounting for about 95% of total wine production in the region), most made primarily from the Syrah and Grenache grapes. For its white wines, Viognier, Roussanne, and Marsanne (among others) are used.

THE WINES OF THE RHONE VALLEY

Because of the area's southerly location and its rocky soil, the grapes experience a long, hot growing season, maturing with high levels of sugar (which later will be fermented to a higher alcohol content). For this reason, the Rhône Valley red wines tend to be full, rich, and concentrated and in many cases take a long time to mature.

The appellation *Côte du Rhône* refers to any of over 100 villages in the region, while the more recent *Côtes du Rhône-Villages* refers to seventeen of the best villages, whose name may be shown on the bottle. The *Northern Rhone Valley* includes the northernmost appellation *Côte Rôtie* which produces red wines from the Syrah grape (which is often blended with up to 20% of the white grape Viognier for softness and flavor). These Côte Rôtie wines are aged in wood for three years and need at least a few years in the bottle to soften and become drinkable. *Château Grillet* (the smallest property with its own appellation in France - six acres) produces white wines from the Viognier grape as does the commune *Condrieu*. The communes of *St-Joseph, Crozes-Hermitage* and *Hermitage* produce some white wines from the Roussanne and Marsanne grapes but focus more on red wines from the Syrah grape with Hermitage having the biggest, fullest wine from the area (some able to last fifty years or more). ***Cornas*** also produces heavy wines from the Syrah grape while ***St-Péray*** produces heavy, thick and rich sparkling wines from the Roussanne and Marsanne grapes. The *Southern Rhone Valley* produces almost entirely rosé and red wines, offering what many consider to be the finest rosé of France from the commune of ***Tavel***. A rosé produced from not more than 60% Grenache grapes but at least 15% of the white grape Cinsault, it shows the dryness of a red wine with the fresh lightness of a white. Neighboring ***Lirac*** also produces a rosé similar in style to the Tavel. ***Châteauneuf-du-Pape*** is one of the more famous wines of the district and is produced from up to thirteen varieties of grapes (with the Grenache grape almost always in the majority). Because there is so much latitude in grape selection this blend can vary greatly, often providing the consumer with "what he paid for" as better grapes understandably cost more money. Other appellations in the district include ***Gigondas, Rasteau, Côtes du Ventoux***, and ***Beaume de Venise***, the last offering sweet Muscat wines.

CALIFORNIA WINES

With more than 320,000 vineyard acres currently planted, California produces virtually every style and type of wine. The first to plant vines in the area were the Spanish Missionaries in the late 1760's, but it wasn't until after the arrival of Count Agoston Haraszthy in 1849, that California would begin making wine in earnest. The Count succeeded in convincing the Governor of California, John Downey, of the potential economic benefits of wine production to the state of California, and in 1861 he was sent to Europe to bring back as many possible varieties of European vines as he could gather. He returned with over 100,000 cuttings of more than 300 different *vinifera* vines. In just a few years, his vineyard in Sonoma County had 85,000 developed vines and a nursery with another 460,000 vines. After determining the superior varieties, the Count then distributed them all over the state, setting in motion the development of wine production that would someday become the California wine industry.

Over the next few decades the California winemakers developed their craft, managing by the end of the 19th century to compete seriously in international expositions (and occasionally win). As promising a start as this was, on January 1st, 1919 prohibition became the law of the land, and California wine production screeched to a halt. Many of the vineyards that were successfully producing wine for sale were forced to change their crop to the more saleable table grape, or to a different crop entirely. A few vineyards continued producing wine for sacramental purposes, having a head start on the rest of the industry when prohibition was finally repealed in 1933. California was slow to make its comeback following prohibition, until the 1960's and 1970's ushered in an unexpected period of dramatic growth and international recognition. The changing American lifestyle, with a greater emphasis on health, motivated many people to make the switch to wine, with California wines being accessible and relatively inexpensive. Another factor in California's growing success was The Viticulture and the Oenology Department at the University of California - Davis. Focusing on the science of wine-making (while also teaching its more traditional aspects), the Oenology Department educated many of California's young winemakers, many of whom applied what they learned with great success (the program now attracts students from all over the world).

But it wasn't until 1976 that California would officially be recognized as a world-class wine producer. Stephen Spurrier, an English wine merchant working in Paris, organized a wine-tasting, the competition consisting of four California Chardonnays, four California Cabernets, four White Burgundies, and four Grand Cru Classes Bordeaux to be tasted by nine of Paris' greatest wine palettes (including Pierre Brejoux, the I.N.A.O. Inspector General). A blind tasting determined, to the shock and dismay of the judges, the winners to be Mike Grgich's *1973 Chateau Montelena Chardonnay*, and Warren Winiarski's *1973 Stags' Leap Wine Cellars Cabernet*. This event forever changed the wine world's perception of California, elevating it to world-class status almost overnight.

> *"Let us have wine and women,
> mirth and laughter,
> Sermons and soda-water the day after."*
> Lord Byron

The state of California, with its many climates and micro-climates can approximate almost any viticultural region in the world. From coastal plains to inland valley floors, to mountain slopes and irrigated deserts it is truly a diverse growing area (no less so with a 2,000 foot mountain chain running along most of the coast, providing heavy fog in summer on the ocean side and hot, dry growing conditions on the inland side). California wines generally fall into one of three categories: ***Generic*** (general style wine with borrowed names such as *Chablis, Burgundy, Rhine*, etc.), ***Varietal*** (a wine produced from no less than 75% of a named grape), and ***Proprietary*** (a wine from a specific producer with often a trademarked name). There is no legal rating system for California wines (such as A.O.C. wines in France) but the federal government under the direction of the *Bureau of Alcohol, Tobacco and Firearms* has identified certain areas as **American Viticultural Areas** (AVA's - there are 70 in California) and it is the name of this area that will often be seen on the wine label (such as Russian River or Carneros, for example).

*If a **Specific AVA** is listed on the label at least 85% of the grapes used to produce the wine must come from that area although the winery is not necessarily located within the AVA since many wineries own vineyards in or buy grapes from other areas. The remaining 15% may come from anywhere in the state.

***Varietal** wines must be produced from at least 75% of the named grape (with the appellation **California** requiring that 100% of the grapes be grown in California).

***Produced And Bottled By** indicates that at least 75% of the grapes must be crushed and fermented at the winery listed on the label.

***A Specific Vineyard** named indicates that at least 95% of the grapes must come from that vineyard which must also be located in an AVA.

***Estate Bottled** means that 100% of the grapes used came from the winery's vineyards as well as being from an AVA, and all steps in the winemaking process including bottling occur at a single winery even if the estate owns more than one winery.

***Proprietor Grown** or **Vintner Grown** indicates that 100% of the grapes used must come from vineyards controlled or owned by the bottler with no specific area requirements.

***Vintage Date** indicates that at least 95% of the grapes were grown in the year shown, although vintages generally are less important with California wines than some other areas of the world because of the state's less erratic weather.

***Meritage** indicates a blend of wine produced from any or all of the following grapes: (For red wines) *Cabernet Sauvignon, Merlot, Cabernet Franc, Malbec, and Petit Verdot* with some more famous red Meritage wines being *Opus One, Marlstone, Insignia,* and *Dominus,* and (for white wines) *Sauvignon Blanc, Sémillon, Muscadelle, and Savignan Musque*.

If a wine is a blend produced from grapes other than the specific Meritage varieties the winemaker will often create a **Proprietary Name** such as *Ca'del Solo, Il Pescatore,* or *Vin du Mistral.* This name indicates a unique blend of wine although it has no specific legal meaning - the term *"Reserve"* also has no legal meaning but, unlike many proprietary names which are trademarked, it may be used by anyone.

The major winemaking regions of California are: The North Coast (including Napa Valley, Sonoma County, Mendocino County, and Lake County), the North and South Central Coasts (including Monterey County, Santa Clara County, Almeda County, San Luis Obispo, and Santa Barbara County) and the Great Central Valley (including Modesto and the San Joaquin Valley).

NORTH COAST:

NAPA VALLEY is a concentrated vineyard area north of San Fransisco with three distinct growing areas (the coolest to the south where the ocean has a greater influence). It is a popular tourist attraction because of its many vineyards and its considerable natural beauty. Some of the more important AVA's (and vineyards) are:

Rutherford (*Grgich Hills, Beaulieu Vineyards, Franciscan*),

Oakville (*Robert Mondavi, Opus One, Caymus, Far Niente, Cakebread*),

Howell Mountain (*Dunn, Chateau Woltner* - owned by the former owners of Château Haut-Brion in Bordeaux),

Carneros (this AVA being split between Napa and Sonoma Valleys - *Acacia, Domaine Carneros, Saintsbury*),
Stags Leap District (*Stag's Leap Wine Cellars, Stags' Leap Winery, Robert Sinskey, Chimney Rock*) and
Mount Veeder (*Hess Collection, Mayacamas, Mount Veeder Winery*).

SONOMA COUNTY, located Northwest of San Fransisco, is larger than Napa Valley and more diverse, with its countryside a patchwork of vineyards, ranches, orchards, and woodlands. Less touristy with more of a small town feel. Some of its important AVA's (and vineyards) are:
Carneros (*Buena Vista, Gloria Ferrar, Sonoma Creek*),
Alexander Valley (*Jordan, Geyser Peak, Simi*),
Russian River Valley (*Sonoma Cutrer, Rodney Strong, Iron Horse*), and
Dry Creek Valley (*Ferrari Carano, Dry Creek Vineyard*).

MENDOCINO COUNTY is the northernmost winemaking region of importance. Generally it as a cooler wine growing area except for some sections which are sheltered from the fog. Two important AVA's are:

Anderson Valley (*Navarro Vineyards, Kendall Jackson* (having one vineyard in the area), and
McDowell Valley (home to *McDowell Valley Vineyards* exclusively).

LAKE COUNTY is east of Mendocino with most of its vineyards concentrated in the south.

Guenoc Valley is an AVA and home to *Guenoc Vineyards*.

NORTH CENTRAL COAST:

MONTEREY COUNTY received little winemaking attention (because of its low rainfall and chilly ocean winds) until the early 1960's when the increasing demand for California wines required it. The growing season is long and cool with the area water-fed by the underground Salinas River. Home to many small AVA's, noteworthy vineyards include *Estancia, Chalone, Jekel*, and *Monterey Vineyard*.

SANTA CLARA COUNTY is located southeast of San Fransisco and includes the Santa Clara Valley and the foothills of the Santa Cruz Mountains. Home to *J. Lohr Winery* and *Mount Eden Vineyards*.

ALMEDA COUNTY, located just east of San Fransisco, provides a gravelly soil with good drainage and an east-west orientation allow-

ing for the easy flow of Pacific Ocean breezes. Home to the AVA
Livermore Valley (*Livermore Valley Cellars*).
SOUTH CENTRAL COAST: San Luis Obispo and Santa Barbara counties, although quite far south, have cool enough microclimates to produce high quality varietal wines.

SAN LUIS OBISPO includes the AVA
Edna Valley (*Edna Valley Vineyards*) and

SANTA BARBARA COUNTY is home to the AVA's
Santa Maria Valley (*Au Bon Climat, Qupe Cellars, Byron*), and
Santa Ynez Valley (*Firestone Vineyard, Sanford Winery, Santa Barbara Winery, Zaca Mesa Winery*).
GREAT CENTRAL VALLEY:

MODESTO and ***SAN JOAQUIN VALLEY***, this area produces more California wine (mostly "jug" wine) than any other area of the state with more than 50% of California's grapes planted here.

ITALIAN WINES

Italy is the world's largest producer of wine, making all types including red, white, dessert, and sparkling wines (with Asti Spumanti being its most famous sparkling wine), although red wines are this country's primary focus in part because of its more southernly location. Italy has been making wines for more than 3,000 years, and the country is so filled with vineyards that it has been described as no country at all, but instead, one vast vineyard. Over the centuries, wine has been a local affair or even a family affair in Italy. To many Italians, wine is a simple, uncomplicated, everyday beverage (this casual attitude may exist in part because of the generosity of Nature), although there are many producers who take their craft very seriously and who are responsible for some of the world's best wines.

> *"One barrel of wine can work more miracles than a church full of saints."*
> Italian Proverb

The wine law of 1963 created the legal system with which the Italian wine industry must comply. Started in the interest of protecting Italian wine from fraudulent claims and unfair competition (for example, the process of adding sugar to the "must" to increase alcohol content, called chaptalization, is outlawed and easily enforced as the government distributes sugar), the law provides for three levels of classification:

Vino da Tavola (Table Wine): A wine having few restrictions on alcohol content, area of origin, etc., (and may state the name of a region on its label).

Denominazione di Origine Controllata (D.O.C.): This classification controls each regions geographical limits (label must state origin), which grape varieties may be used and their respective percentages, wine production per acre, the minimum alcohol content, and wine aging requirements. There are more than 200 D.O.C. wines accounting for 12% of Italy's total wine production.

Denominazione di Origine Controllata e Garantita (D.O.C.G.): This classification guarantees superior quality through tasting control boards. Its restrictions are the same as above but more stringent. The producer is required to affix a government seal (which is broken as the wine is opened by the consumer) to all D.O.C.G. wines he bottles. Government inspectors may test and analyze the wine at any time, and the label must state origin of wine, name of grower and bottler, place of bottling, and alcoholic strength. The first five wines to qualify for the D.O.C.G. rating were *Barbaresco, Barolo, Brunello di Montalcino, Chianti, and Vino Nobile di Montepulciano*.

Because of the many restrictions associated with becoming a D.O.C. or D.O.C.G. wine, compliance essentially "freezes" a wine's style making continued experimentation difficult. Many excellent Italian wines have only a Vino da Tavola (Table Wine) rating because they fail to meet one or more of the D.O.C. guidelines (for example, *Sassicaia*, a Tuscan 100% Cabernet

Sauvignon created by Piero Antinori was for many years a simple table wine but finally won its own appellation ***Bolgheri Russo*** - 80% Cabernet Sauvignon minimum with the addition of Merlot and Sangiovese allowed). There are literally hundreds of grapes used in the production of Italian wines but the two most prevalent are the red grapes Sangiovese (the primary grape in Chianti) and Nebbiolo (used for the heavier Barolos and Barbarescos).

Italy is broken into twenty wine-producing regions with ninety-three provinces and more than 2300 wine labels. Italian wines are generally labeled by either the ***Region of Origin*** (Chianti Classico, for example), ***Proprietary Name*** (such as Sassicaia), or the ***Principal Grape*** used (for example, Nebbiolo d'Alba). Of the twenty regions of Italy, three of the more important are: Tuscany, Piedmont, and Veneto.

TUSCANY: The biggest and most complex D.O.C. area in Italy. Sangiovese is the most prevalent grape and Chianti is its most famous wine. ***Chianti***: Considered one of the better wines of Italy, it is produced in one of three quality levels:

*****Chianti***, the most basic,

Chianti Classico, from the best of seven zones producing Chianti, and
Chianti Classico Riserva, Chianti Classico aged for three years.
1967 guidelines for D.O.C. Chianti allow for a blend of 50 to 80% Sangiovese, 10 to 30% Canaiolo (red) and 10 to 30% Trebbiano and Malvasia Grapes (white). D.O.C.G. Chiantis require a minimum of 80% Sangiovese with a mere 2% minimum for white grapes and up to 10% optional grapes. Two of the more frequently seen producers of Chianti are *Antinori* and *Ruffino*. Other quality red wines from Tuscany include **Brunello di Montalcino** produced from the Sangiovese grape, a wine that will require age - at least five to ten years with better examples needing up to twenty years, and **Vino Nobile di Montepulciano** (similar to Chianti in grapes allowed with some latitude for local grapes and a minimum of two years in wood, with **Riserva** requiring three years in wood, and **Riserva Speciale**, four years).

PIEDMONT: The name of this region originates from "a pie del monti" or "at the foot of the mountains." From a series of valleys and fertile plains to the hills of Monferrato, Piedmont produces some of Italy's fullest, richest red wines. ***Barolo*** is the name of one of Italy's finest red wines and the name of the city around which the wine's Nebbiolo grapes are grown. In the area this wine is known as the wine of kings and the king of wines. It is big, rich and complex, and high in alcohol and tannin. All Barolos must spend at least two years in wood and be aged no less than three years total. ***Barolo Riserva*** must be aged four years, and ***Barolo Riserva Speciale***, at least five years. ***Barbaresco*** wines are from the area around the town of Barbaresco northeast of Barolo, and it too is made from the Nebbiolo grape. Different soils produce different grapes though, and Barbaresco is softer and less alcoholic than Barolo (and is required to have only two years aging, one in wood, with ***Barbaresco Riserva*** requiring three years, and ***Barbaresco Riserva Speciale***, four years). Both Barolo and Barbaresco are D.O.C.G. wines, with two of its more recognizable producers being *Fontanafredda* and *Gaja*.

VENETO: One of Italy's largest wine-producing regions and home to the houses of Capulet and Montague (referred to in Shakespeare's Romeo and Juliet), and the place where the author of The Divine Comedy, Dante Alighieri, found refuge. It is also home to what can be two of Italy's better blended light red table wines, **Valpolicella** and **Bardolino** (both made from Corvina Veronese, Rondinella, and Molinara grapes). These wines are best consumed young, generally the younger the better. **Soave** and **Pinot Grigio** are two of Veneto's (and Italy's) more famous white wines, and are generally light, smooth, and refreshing. Another of Veneto's more famous wines is **Recioto della Valpolicella-Amarone**. *Amarone* is produced from only the ripest grapes from each bunch (the same type of grapes as for Valpolicella, but which may also be affected by *Noble Rot*), which are left to dry or raisinate on reed trays for three months then vinified with no residual sugar, making a rich, dry, slightly bitter wine that is high in alcohol (14 - 16%). Some consider it one of Italy's greatest red wines.

> *"Boy, bring wine and dice. Let tomorrow seek its own salvation! Death, twitching the ear, cries: Enjoy your life: I come!"*
> *Virgil from "The Copa"*

GERMAN WINES

There are more than 1400 villages in Germany with over 2600 vineyards occupying some 240,000 acres. There are approximately 100,000 growers with the average holding only 2.4 acres. The minimum acreage for a vineyard is 12.5 acres (as of 1971 when the German government greatly simplified the organization of property) so many vineyards have more than one owner. The Romans were the first to plant vines and German wines have enjoyed fame as far back as Charlemagne (800 AD). The monasteries helped to develop and spread the popularity of wine, and today German culture is greatly influenced by its wines and wine production.

Germany is the northernmost country in which vines will grow, and it produces about 2 to 3% of the world's wine which tends to be lower in alcohol. 80% of German vines are on slopes, some of which are very steep making harvesting difficult, with the best vineyards having a southern exposure. 85% of German wine production is white wine as most red grapes don't grow well in its cooler climate. Although there is a general lack of heat the growing season tends to be longer, and the longer the grapes stay on the vine the sweeter they become ("100 days makes good wine, 120 days makes great wine" as the saying goes - although the later into the season the grapes remain on the vine the greater the risk of bad weather damaging or destroying the grapes). If the grapes do not receive enough sun or if the growing season is a short one, sugar may be added to the "must" to boost the alcohol content (***Chaptalization***), although this is not allowed in higher quality German wines. Most German wines are fermented dry (no sugar remaining after fermentation) but a specific amount of unfermented juice (***Süss-Reserve***) may be held back, which may then be added to the wine after fermentation to sweeten it. Any German ***Varietal*** wine must be produced from at least 85% of the named variety, and a particular ***Vintage*** indicates that at least 85% of the grapes came from the named year (vintages are very important to German wines due to the unpredictable weather with 1976 and 1988 being the best years since 1949).

The primary grapes used in the production of German wine are Riesling (the most important), Silvaner, Müller-Thurgau (a combination of two Riesling clones and the most widely planted grape), and Gewürztraminer, among many other less common grapes. There are eleven important winemaking regions in Germany found in the valleys of the Rhine and Mosel rivers and their tributaries: *Mosel-Saar-Ruwer, Rheingau, Rheinhessen, Pfalz* (these first four are where most of the German wines found in the U.S. originate), *Nahe, Mittelrhein, Ahr, Hessische Bergstrasse, Franken, Württemberg, and Bade*. Additionally, there are two small formally East German wine-producing areas that now fall under the 1971 German Wine Law: *Saale-Unstrut* and *Sachsen*. Important villages in the *Mosel-Saar-Ruwer* include *Bernkastel, Piesport, Graach*, and *Wehlen* and some of the important vineyards are *Bernkasteler Doktor, Piesporter Goldtröpfchen, Wehlener Sonnenuhr*, and *Graacher-Himmelreich* (when er is added to a German word it means "from that place" as someone from New York would be called a New Yorker). Mosel wines tend to be higher in acid and lower in alcohol (sometimes with a slight sparkle) and are always sold in green bottles. In the **Rheingau**, important villages include *Johannisberg, Eltville, Erbach*, and *Rüdesheim* with a few important vineyards being *Scloss Johannisberg, Scloss Vollrads*, and *Steinberg*. Rhein wines generally have more body than Mosel wines, and are always sold in brown bottles.

> *If a German wine is bottled by the producer the label will state "Erzeugerabfüllung" (bottled by producer) or "Aus Eigenem lesegut" (from his own grapes), and is similar to Estate Bottling in France. If the shipper bottles a wine coming from a particular estate then the label will read "Aus Dem Lesegut Von & the Estate name" (out of the harvest of).*

German wines are broken down into four general quality levels with the highest level further broken down into six additional classifications.

Deutsche Tafelwein (German Table Wine) is the first or lowest designation indicating a wine from any of the accepted grapes from any of the four Tafelwein regions (if the label does not read Deutsche the wine may come from other European countries, usually Italy, and may be altered with the addition of *Süss-Reserve* to approximate the German style).

Landwein, the second designation requires a higher concentration of grape sugar, and the grapes must originate in one of twenty specific areas and is either dry (*Trocken*) or semi-dry (*Halb-Trocken*).

__Qualitätswein bestimmter Anbaugebiete__ (Q.b.A.), the third designation, indicates wines produced from accepted grape varieties, and originating in one of eleven specific regions (mentioned earlier). These wines may be chaptalized and must pass a lab test and official tasting to receive a control number prior to release.

__Qualitätswein Mit Prädikat__ (Prädikat or Q.m.P) is the same as Q.b.A. with one very important difference: Prädikat wines may ***not*** be chaptalized. Prädikat wines represent the best of German wines and are further classified as to their grape's maturity (and so to the sweetness of the finished wine also).

__Kabinett__ indicates wine produced from normally ripened grapes.

Spätlese indicates wines produced from riper grapes picked after normal harvest, or from grapes with extra ripeness picked during normal harvest, both of which may be affected by *Noble Rot* (a desirable mold which may grow on grapes, having the effect of concentrating their sugar).

Auslese is wine produced from selectively picked bunches of grapes which show particular ripeness and may also show *Noble Rot*.

Beerenauslese indicates wine produced from individually selected grapes which show exceptional ripeness and usually are affected by *Noble Rot* - these wines are produced only about 2 to 3 times a decade.

Trockenbeerenauslese indicating wines produced from grapes that are shrunken and shriveled by *Noble Rot* (representing the richest, sweetest, most expensive wines of Germany).

Eiswein is the final classification, and is somewhat different than the others. It indicates wine made from grapes frozen on the vine, which are pressed before thawing, separating the frozen water from the grapes' sugars and acids. The minimum sugar level is the same as that for Beerenauslese and the cost can vary depending on the grapes used. Because of this wine's high acid content it will age very well, lasting almost indefinitely.

> *"Never apologize for, or be ashamed of, your own taste in wine. Preferences for wines vary just as much as those for art or music."*
> *Humbrecht Duijker*

AUSTRALIAN WINES

With more than 700 wineries spread out over the southern portion of the continent, Australia produces all varieties of wines with approximately two thirds of its vineyards planted with white grapes. The major white grape varieties grown include Rhine Riesling, Sémillon, and Chardonnay and the major red grapes are Shiraz (Syrah), Cabernet Sauvignon, and Pinot Noir. Grape cultivation started in 1788 with Captain Arthur Phillip bringing vine cuttings in from Rio de Janeiro and the Cape of Good Hope. Gregory Blaxland and John MacArthur began vineyards in the early 1800's and James Busby, arriving from Scotland in 1824, taught viticulture and planted 678 varieties of vines from France, Spain, England and Luxembourg. Many Australian wineries are still owned by the same families that started them over a century ago.

There is no national labeling system for Australian wines, such as A.O.C. wines in France, but the various states regulate wine labels as to the *Grape Variety* (a minimum of 80% of the named grape, and if it is a blend then the respective percentages must be listed); *Region* (a minimum of 80% must come from the district named); and *Vintage* (the wine must be produced from at least 95% of grapes from the named year). The *Bin #* found on many Australian wine labels indicates a particular wine style. There are thirty specific wine growing regions in Australia further broken into approximately eighty districts and subdistricts. Of the six states of Australia the more important wine-producing areas include*:*

NEW SOUTH WALES with its *Hunter Valley* (famous for its Shiraz and Sémillion wines, it also produces Chardonnays and Cabernets) and *Mudgee* (the growers here having their own self-imposed appellation system),

SOUTH AUSTRALIA with its *Barossa Valley* (the oldest wine district, first settled by the Germans, offering quality Rieslings as well as all other types of Australian wines), *Coonawarra* (offering premium red wines), *Southern Vales, Adelaide Hill and Clare*,

VICTORIA with its ***Yarra Valley*** (home to many excellent "Boutique" wineries), ***Rutherglew, Great Western, and Goulburn Valley***, and
WESTERN AUSTRALIA offering wines from ***Frankland, Margaret River and Great Southern***.

Some of the best Australian wineries include *Brown Brothers, Lindeman, Penfolds, Rosemount, Wolf Blass, Seppelt, and Petaluma.*

> *"If penicillin can cure those who are ill, Spanish sherry can bring the dead back to life."*
> **Sir Alexander Fleming**

SHERRY

Sherry is produced in Andalucía, Spain in the Sherry Zone, a growing area of some 50,000 acres located between the Guadalquivir and Guadalete Rivers, near the three towns of Jerez de la Frontera, Puerto do Santa María, and Sanlúcar de Barrameda. Accounting for only 3% of Spain's wine production, sherry is a fortified wine (wine that has brandy added to it, in this case, after fermentation is completed). Primary grapes used in the production of sherry are the Palomino grape (90% of the grapes planted in the Sherry zone) and Pedro Ximénex (said to named after Peter Siemons, the man who first brought the grape to Sherry from Germany). Sherry is subjected to what is called "controlled oxidation" (exposure to air - unlike most wines which are protected from this) in oak barrels that are kept only about two thirds full and stored with a loosely fitting cork. There is no such thing as a vintage sherry as all is blended, sometimes with as many as ten to twenty vintages, in what is referred to as a "Solera System." If a date is shown on a Sherry bottle it indicates only the year the solera was established, and not the vintage of the wine.

The Solera System is a fractional blending and aging process involving the use of barrels (called "butts") made of American white oak which are stacked in such a way as to group the first vintage butts (called the solera) side-by-side in a *bodega* or above ground wine storage area. The following year an equal number of butts from the second year vintage (called the first criadera) are stacked on top of the solera butts, and the year after that the third year vintage butts (the second criadera) are stacked above the first criadera. Additional criaderas may be set aside to back up the other three sometimes with as many as twelve criaderas to a solera system. After the system is complete, once a year the foreman of the bodega removes no more than one-third of the wine from each of the oldest or solera butts for bottling and sale, and refills them with wine taken from each of the first criadera butts. These in turn are refilled from the second criadera butts and so on until the youngest criadera is refilled with fresh wine that best matches the style of its elders. This system of transfer allows for the continuous aging of the wine on all levels with each criadera and the solera maintaining its integrity as no more than one third of the wine is removed each year (allowing for a consistent product).

There are three basic styles of sherry: Fino Style (including the types Fino, Manzanilla, and Amontillado), Oloroso Style (including the types Oloroso and Cream), and Pedro Ximénex Sherry.

FINO STYLE SHERRY is produced by fermenting the "must" of (usually) Palomino grapes and allowing for the development of a "Flor" (a flowering of yeast on the surface of the wine, usually heavier in spring and fall - a phenomenon unique to only three other areas of the world: Russia, South Africa and France's Jura Mountains). If a lighter, pale-colored wine with a particularly thick "flor" layer develops it will be lightly fortified with brandy to an alcohol level of about 15% and will eventually become, if produced in Jerez, a ***Fino Type Sherry*** (very light and dry and pale in color) and, if it is produced in

Sanlúcar, it will become a **Manzanilla Type Sherry** (also very light and dry but with a slightly salty taste as Sanlúcar is located on the coast where the Atlantic Ocean air influences its development). If the" flor" does not maintain itself and eventually dies off the wine will be fortified with brandy to about 18% and will become an **Amontillado Type Sherry** (deeper colored with more body - usually dry).

    OLOROSO STYLE SHERRY is produced from the "must" of (usually) Palomino grapes that have been sun-dried for twelve to twenty-four hours (concentrating sugar by evaporating the grape's water). *Oloroso Type Sherry* is produced with no "flor" and fortified to about 18% and when finished has a deep golden color, more body and is usually sweet. Older, richer Olorosos combined with Pedro Ximénex sherry produce **Cream Type Sherry** (even sweeter) and *Pale Cream Sherry* is produced from a combination of Fino and Pedro Ximénex sherries.

    PEDRO XIMÉNEX SHERRY is produced from Pedro Ximénex grapes that have been sun-dried for ten to fourteen days. The must is not allowed to ferment (its syrupy nature would require too much time) but instead is placed in butts containing brandy and allowed to age in its own solera system. Pedro Ximénex sherry is very thick, dark and syrupy sweet.

Some of the top sherry producers are *Sandeman, González Byass, Harvey's, Williams and Humbert, Pedro Domecq, and Croft.* Four of the top-selling Sherries are *Bristol Cream, Dry Sack, Tío Pepe, and La Ina.*

PORT

Produced in the Douro region in Northern Portugal, Port is a fortified wine (a wine with brandy added, in this case, *during* fermentation which arrests the process giving the wine a residual sugar level of about 9 to 11%, and an alcohol level of about 20% when finished). Port is usually a blended wine, often of six or seven grapes with up to eighty varieties allowed, of which there are two basic styles: Wood Port and Vintage Port.

***Wood Port** is matured in wood and ready to drink when bottled, and is produced in two styles:

Ruby Port is blended from young non-vintage ports and aged at least three years before shipping. It is dark purple in color, sweet and fruity.

Tawny Port is a blend of mature wooded ports aged in casks for up to forty years (although the minimum age requirement is only three years). It is more delicate and lighter than ruby port, with older tawnies being more expensive, and usually drier (relatively speaking) than the younger ones.

*****Vintage Port*** is a port that is blended from the grapes of an exceptional year with a minimum of twenty-two and a maximum of thirty-one months in wood, and a port which will continue to improve in the bottle, taking as long as fifteen to thirty years to fully mature. Vintage port has a deep purple color and is very fruity with exceptional body, and will require decanting as it throws quite alot of sediment over its years of bottle aging. The decision to declare a particular year a vintage year is made by the individual shipper (occurring about three times a decade with some of the best vintages being 1963, 1970, 1977, 1983, 1985, 1991, and 1992).

Late Bottled Vintage (LBV) indicates a wood port produced from a the grapes of a single year, unblended and aged three and a half to six years in wood barrels. Lighter in flavor and color than vintage port, it is ready to drink when bottled and will not require decanting.

> *"Give me wine to wash me clean
> From the weather-stains of care."*
> Ralph Waldo Emerson

Vintage Character (Vintage Release) is a quality port similar to LBV port but instead is a blend of better vintages that have been kept in wood for four to five years.

Colheita Port is a single vintage tawny port aged for a minimum of seven years.

Single Quinta (Vineyard) Ports are produced from the best grapes of a particular *quinta* from a year that was not quite good enough to be declared a vintage year. These ports will age in wood for two to three years, receiving additional aging in the bottle prior to release, and can be consumed when purchased (and probably will require decanting).

White Port is a port produced from white grape varieties usually fermented longer before the addition of brandy (rendering it a little drier) and is meant to be drunk as an aperitif rather than as a dessert wine. Some of the top producers of ports include *Cockburn, Fonseca, Warre & Co., Dow, Croft, W. & J. Graham, Sandeman, Taylor Fladgate, and Quinto do Noval.*

BEER

Fundamentally, beer is a beverage obtained from the fermentation of grains, which is also usually flavored with hops. Beer has been with Mankind for thousands of years in all civilizations. The Egyptians made reference to brewing in their hieroglyphics, and the Russians, Chinese, and Japanese all have beers of ancient origin. Today there is a tremendous variety of beers worldwide, with the United States alone having more than 400 breweries producing in excess of 1000 different types of beer. There are four fundamental ingredients which are essential to quality beer: water, grains, yeast, and hops.

*Water is tremendously important as it comprises up to 90% of the finished beer and is used in all areas of the brewing process. Early breweries were located near a source of clean appropriate water for brewing, as quality beer production would be impossible without it. Today, water

can be chemically analyzed and adjusted by the brewer to fit his needs, so the brewery's location is no longer as important as it once was.

Grains are the essential ingredients from which beer is produced. Malted barley is the most common grain used, being a major component in almost all beer styles, offering a sweet, soft flavor and aroma. Wheat is used in conjunction with barley to produce a light refreshing beer. Corn and rice are common additions to beer, particularly in the United States, contributing a clean crispness to the finished product. Oats may be used (usually in specialty beers) giving the beer an oily smoothness, and rye is sometimes used to give the beer a slightly spicy flavor.

Yeast: In 1883, Emil Hansen of the Carlsberg Brewery in Denmark succeeded in isolating single cell yeast strains, providing for future brewers much more control over a very important part of the brewing process. Each individual strain of yeast contributes unique characteristics to the finished beer and most breweries maintain sterile brewing environments so as not to introduce wild yeast strains or other micro-organisms which may harm the carefully selected brewing yeasts.

Hops: The female hop vine produces a cone-like flower which has been associated with beer production since the 12th century, coming into general use in the 14th century. Hops contribute a pleasant bitter, herbal flavor and an antiseptic quality that discourages the growth of bacteria which may contaminate the future beer.

The Brewing Process: Barley, the primary grain used in beer production, is generally malted, a process whereby the grain is soaked in water for a day or two, then allowed to germinate or sprout for a week or longer. The grain is now referred to as "malt" or "malted" as it has been allowed to germinate. Malting releases enzymes in the grain which convert unfermentable starches into sugars (corn and rice cannot be malted but are instead cooked to soften their cellular structure, and later mixed with the malted barley). After germination has reached the proper point, the malt is kiln-dried to arrest the germination process, and to determine the flavor and color of the finished beer (light roasting yields a lighter crisper beer, while heavy roasting makes for a darker, fuller-flavored beer). The malt is then ground and mixed with other grains (if desired) in the mash tub, where hot water is added and the mixture is allowed to stand, continuing the conversion of starches to sugars. When the water has absorbed all it can from the grains, it is strained off (now referred to as "wort") and moved to the brewing kettle. Here, hops are added and the wort is boiled to sterilize and purify it, and complete the conversion of starch to sugar. Following brewing, the wort is strained to remove the hops and moved to the fermenting vat. Here yeast of very specific strains are added (which will greatly influence the quality of the finished beer), and the wort is allowed to ferment. Lagers employ a lower temperature bottom-fermenting yeast, which thoroughly converts the sugar to alcohol producing a cleaner, crisper beer, while ales use a higher temperature top-fermenting yeast which is often less efficient, leaving behind sugars which impart to the finished ale a fruity flavor and aroma. If the beer is to be aged or *lagered* it is allowed to rest for weeks or months at near freezing temperatures so that yeast impurities may settle, flavors may soften and improve, and a slow second fermentation may occur. *Krausening* may also be used to carbonate beer, a process whereby a small amount of partially fermented brew is added to the beer to induce a second fermentation. Following carbonation, the beer is filtered, and may be pasteurized to kill any remaining live yeast (so bottles or cans won't burst from additional fermentation) and then packaged.

Because beer is a worldwide phenomenon, produced in a wide variety of styles, it is difficult to categorize. Listed below are some of the more common styles:

Lager: A bottom-fermented beer which has been aged or "rested" near freezing for weeks to months. A light, clean, refreshing beer.

Pilsner: The only true pilsner beer is *Pilsner Urquell* form Pilsen, Czechoslovakia. Use of the name "Pilsner" in describing a beer indicates a light, hoppy, dry lager.

Bock: A strong dark lager with a malty sweetness. Doublebocks are also produced (often seasonally), showing heavier bock characteristics.

Ale: A top-fermented beer which is usually full bodied with fruity aromas and more complex flavors than a lager.

> ***Mild:*** An ale which is light in body and low in alcohol, but often full flavored.
>
> ***Bitter:*** As the name implies, a bitter beer, usually stronger than a mild and quite dry (hoppy).
>
> ***Pale Ale:*** Less hoppy than a bitter, with reddish tones and a light, fresh flavor.
>
> ***Brown Ale:*** A strong malty beer with

deep color and a nutty flavor - sometimes sweet.

Old Ale: Very deep in color and flavor, usually sweet.

Scottish Ale: A full bodied malty beer, with peat undertones. Sometimes not fully fermented, so it can be lower in alcohol.

Steam beer is a unique style of beer, the name having originated with the highly carbonated beers produced locally on the west coast at the end of the 19th century. When a keg of steam beer was tapped it would release a large amount of carbon dioxide, much like steam rising from a steam engine. Anchor Brewing Co. of San Francisco produces "Anchor Steam," a beer brewed in the traditional style, that is, a beer fermented with lager yeast (bottom-fermenting) at ale yeast temperatures. It possesses the light crispness of a lager while also having the richness and fruitiness of an ale.

Porter/Stout: These beers are usually ales. Produced from heavily roasted barley, they are often almost black in color, and full and rich in flavor. Stouts are the darker and richer of the two although the alcohol content is often similar.

Barleywine: The strongest of beers. Barleywine is an ale which can vary in color, but is always heavy, malty, and fruity. Traditionally matured in wood casks.

Wheat Beer: Usually an ale, it is produced from barley with the addition of wheat. A light, carbonated, refreshing beer. In Germany, they are referred to as Weizenbier (wheat beer) or Weisse (white) Beer.

Trappist Beer: An ale produced in a Trappist monastery. There are only six such breweries entitled to this appellation of origin, producing some twenty different beers. In general, a strong beer, rich with yeast sediment, aromatic, and fruity.

Lambic: A tart, dry, earthy beer. A lambic is an ale produced from malted barley with the addition of at least 30% wheat. All lambics are naturally fermented by wild yeasts, imparting a unique flavor to each batch of beer. They may also have sugar or fruit (usually cherries or raspberries) added after fermentation. Some are still (non-carbonated) while others are naturally carbonated. Lambic styles have changed little over the past 400 years.

SPIRITS IN GENERAL

Spirits have been with mankind for nearly 3000 years in various cultures and on various continents. The Chinese were producing a spirit from rice beer in 800 B.C. and Aristotle, in the 4th century B.C. made mention of distillation in his work *Meteorology*. Through the centuries, techniques and styles associated with the production of spirits have greatly improved, today providing the world with many highly refined and subtle alcoholic beverages. The major classifications of spirits are Whiskey (a grain product), Vodka (produced from various grains, potatoes, beets or molasses), Gin (neutral spirits with flavorings), Rum (produced from sugarcane by-products), Tequila (the mezcal plant), Brandy (obtained from grapes), and Liqueurs (produced from various sources which are flavored and always sweetened).

WHAT IS DISTILLATION?

The process whereby water is removed from a previously fermented liquid rendering a more potent or condensed alcoholic beverage generally referred to as a spirit (for example, wine subjected to distillation becomes brandy, and beer becomes whiskey). This is possible because ethyl alcohol boils at 173° while water boils at 212.° Applying heat above 173° but below 212° allows for the separation of ethyl alcohol, along with certain flavor compounds, from the original liquid. If this alcohol vapor is captured through the use of a still (which recondenses the vapor to a liquid) a new alcoholic beverage is created.

There are two basic types of stills: The pot still and the continuous still. The pot still is a single batch distilling device almost always made of copper as copper removes certain impurities from the alcohol during the distillation process. The pot still is preferred for the production of high quality spirits as it better transfers flavors and fragrances to the finished spirit (for centuries spirits were the result of a single distillation process until the 16th century when the practice of redistilling a spirit came into being - with each successive distillation, additional water and flavoring agents are removed eventually rendering an almost pure alcohol product referred to as "neutral spirits"). The continuous still, as its name implies, is a still which will provide a continuous stream of spirit as long as a fermented beverage is added to it. Invented in the 1820's, it is preferred for larger spirits production where subtlety is not as important. It is cheaper, faster, and capable of more easily producing pure spirits.

The term proof, in referring to spirits, indicates alcoholic strength. Early distillers determined alcoholic strength by applying a flame to a mixture of gunpowder and spirit. If it ignited and burned with a steady blue flame it was referred to as "proved" (if it failed to ignite, the spirit was "underproof" and if it burned too brightly it was "overproof"). This "proved" spirit was approximately 50% alcohol by volume, and today proof in the United States is expressed as twice the alcohol by volume (for example, most whiskies are between 40 - 43% alcohol by volume and are labeled at 80 - 86 proof, and neutral spirits, produced at 97% alcohol by volume, are labeled at 194 proof).

WHISKEY

Whiskey is a spirit produced from grain and aged, often for years, in new and used wood barrels usually made of oak. The four major whiskey producing countries of the world are Scotland, Ireland, the United States, and Canada. Ireland was the first country to have its whiskey exported around the world, but after phylloxera destroyed many of the vineyards in France in the 1870's (limiting Cognac production), Scotland entered the world stage and has dominated the whiskey trade ever since.

Although production styles and techniques vary from country to country (and area to area) the following procedures are common to all whiskey production. *Malting*: The cereal grain (in Scotland, barley, and elsewhere sometimes rye) is soaked in water and allowed to germinate or sprout. This process activates enzymes which convert the unfermentable starches into sugars. The grain is now referred to as "malt" or "malted" as it has been allowed to germinate. The malting process is stopped by hot air kilning (in Scotland, peat fires are used to arrest germination which contributes greatly to the flavor of the finished whiskey) and the grain is ground to facilitate the coming procedures. If the grain is not malted, as is the case with corn and other grains intended to become simple grain whiskey, it will instead be cooked. *Cooking* breaks down the grain's unfermentable starches, with barley malt added after cooking to contribute its enzyme action and complete the conversion of starch to sugar. *Mashing*: The grain(s) are mixed with warm water in a "mash tub" and allowed to "rest" until all starch has been converted to fermentable sugar. When the water has absorbed all it can from the grain(s) it is drawn off and cooled (now referred to as "wort"). *Fermentation*: The wort is subjected to fermentation through the action of selected yeasts in either wood or stainless steel vats. *Distillation*: Malt whiskies are distilled in pot stills (twice in Scotland and three times in Ireland) while grain whiskies are usually distilled in continuous stills.

SCOTLAND: Although there is no definitive classification of Scotch whisky it is generally agreed that there are four major whisky producing areas in the country:

***The Highlands**, a large and diverse area in the north of Scotland including *Speyside*, the world's finest whisky making region,

***The Lowlands** in the south of Scotland,

***Cambeltown** in the southwest corner of the country, and

***Islay**, an island just off the southwest coast.

Other areas include the **Western Isles *(Jura, Mull, and Skye)*** and the **Orkney Islands** to the north. Scotch whisky is unique as to its water which runs freely in Scotland's many rivers, and to the peat fuel used to stop the germination of the barley which contributes a pleasant smoky, peaty flavor. Scotland has vastly more whisky distilleries than any other country in the world and its whisky is an undeniable part of the country's identity.

Scotland produces three styles of whisky: single malt, vatted and blended.

****Single Malt Whisky*** is produced from malted barley and is not blended with any other whisky. It is aged for at least three years, and typically six to twelve years with some aging as long as fifty years. Single malt whiskies are aged in new or used wood barrels, often American white oak barrels previously used in bourbon production or, in used sherry casks which will impart a sweeter flavor to the whisky. These barrels may be reused up to three times, becoming more subtle in their contributions with each successive use.

> *Age in itself does not necessarily indicate quality in a whisky, but indicates instead the amount of time the producer felt the particular whisky needed to mature.*

Highland Single Malt Whiskies, although diverse and numerous, tend to light elegance with a slightly smoky flavor, while *Lowland Single Malts* are generally softer and lighter in flavor and body. Both Highland and Lowland single malts receive less peat kilning and are generally aged between six and eight years. *Cambeltown Single Malts* (only two distilleries remain) are heavy and smoky with a slight brine flavor while *Islay Single Malts* (seven distilleries) are exceptionally smoky with a stronger brine flavor. Cambeltown and Islay single malts generally receive heavy peat kilning and are influenced by their proximity to the ocean. They generally need about ten to twelve years to mature.

Vatted Malt Whisky is a blend of single malt whiskies and so the same in production as single malts with the additional step of blending. The indication "pure malt" may be used on both a vatted whisky and a single malt (as they both are pure malt whiskies) making it difficult for the consumer to discern between the two, although the major distillers produce only about a dozen vatted whiskies.

* ***Blended Scotch Whisky*** made its debut in 1853 in a successful attempt to broaden the appeal of Scotch whisky by lowering the cost, offering a uniform and consistent product, and softening the rougher edges of malt whisky. Blended Scotch whisky is a combination of malt whiskies and grain whiskies. Grain whiskies, by nature, are less diverse and subtle in character, and so are produced in continuous stills (most of which are located in the Lowlands), and are aged three to four years before blending. The usual blend is between 20 and 50% malt whisky (usually Highland) with the balance being grain whisky, with as many as thirty to forty malts and five or more grain whiskies used in a blend. The age of the whiskies can vary greatly as none is used before

it is mature, with any label statement as to age indicating the youngest in the blend.

IRELAND: Missionary monks, returning from the Middle East, were probably the first to introduce whiskey to Ireland in the 6th century A.D. By the 19th century Irish whiskey enjoyed global dominance, with hundreds of distilleries satisfying the world's taste. Scotch whisky, for a variety of reasons, eventually took over the market, and Ireland now has only three remaining distilleries producing some twenty different varieties and labels. Irish whiskey is usually produced from malted barley, which receives no peat kilning, and unmalted barley (both of which are distilled in pot stills), with the addition of grain whiskey (commonly produced in a continuous still). Irish whiskey is triple distilled, in part because of the strength of its unmalted barley, rendering a lighter, smoother whiskey. The absence of peat separates Irish whiskey from its Scottish counterpart and allows for the sweetness of the barley and the fullness of the malt to come through. By law all Irish whiskey must be aged at least three years (and usually five years), often in used bourbon or sherry casks, and is bottled between 80 and 86 proof.

> *"Actually, it only takes one drink to get me loaded. Trouble is, I can't remember if it's the thirteenth or the fourteenth."*
> George Burns

THE UNITED STATES: Whiskey first came to the United States with the early American settlers, being considered necessary for the arduous ocean voyage and as a medicine in the New World. U.S. whiskey production began in Pennsylvania, Virginia, and Maryland in the 18th century, but in 1791 the government's plan to tax whiskey drove the distillers further into the new country, where they found ideal locations in Indiana and Kentucky (providing both fertile farmland and excellent limestone water). The Reverend Elijah Craig is said to have originated the American whiskey style in Bourbon County, Kentucky, using corn rather than barley as it was more plentiful, calling his whiskey "Bourbon County Whiskey" (the name Bourbon still indicates a corn whiskey).

American whiskey is produced in continuous stills and is subjected to two different yeasting styles: *Sweet mash* which indicates a fermentation induced by the addition of yeast to fresh mash only, and *sour mash* (common to bourbon production) which indicates that at least 1/4 of the mash be from a previous distillation. American whiskey is divided into two major categories: Straight and blended.

***Straight Whiskey** is distilled at no more than 160 proof (a higher proof at distillation indicates a lighter spirit with 160 proof still being quite heavy). It is aged at least two years, and usually four to twelve years, in *new* barrels of charred white oak. It is bottled at no less than 80 proof and the only thing that may be added to straight whiskey to adjust its proof is water. To carry the designation "straight" it must be produced from at least 51% of a specific grain (corn, rye, barley, wheat) and may not be mixed with neutral spirits. If at least 51% of the grain is corn then it is a straight *Bourbon Whiskey*, and if 80% or more is corn and the resulting whiskey is aged in uncharred oak barrels or *used* charred oak barrels, it a straight *Corn Whiskey*. With whiskeys other than corn, if at least 51% is from a particular grain it is designated a straight *Rye Whiskey*, a straight *Wheat whiskey* etc. *Tennessee Whiskey* is a straight whiskey distilled in Tennessee from at least 51% of any particular grain (usually corn). It is aged at least four years and is additionally charcoal treated which removes the lighter flavors and imparts a slight smokiness. *Bottled in Bond* is a tax term indicating that taxes will be deferred until the spirits are shipped and offers no particular guarantee of quality to the consumer. Bottled in Bond whiskeys must be straight whiskeys distilled at no more than 160 proof and bottled at 100 proof, and must be aged at least four years. Straight whiskey may also be mixed and retain its straight whiskey designation as long as it is of whiskeys from the same distillery and distilling period. If the whiskey is from different distilleries or distilling periods the label will indicate blended rye whiskey, blended corn whiskey, etc.

Blended Whiskey must contain at least 20% straight whiskeys and may be mixed with simple grain whiskey and/or neutral spirits (with seventy or more different whiskeys in a blend) and may not carry an indication of a particular grain. Additionally up to 2 1/2 % of the blend may be other blending ingredients such as sherry wine or peach juice.

CANADA: Canadian whisky production began at the end of the 18th century and developed parallel to Canadian grain farming. All Canadian whisky is produced in continuous stills and must be aged a minimum of three years in any of a variety of barrels including new wood and used bourbon, brandy, or sherry casks. Canadian whisky is a blend, often of twenty or more different whiskies and may be produced from cereal grains only (usually corn, rye, wheat, and barley). No more than 50% of any one particular grain may be used so there is no such thing as a Canadian straight whisky. Most Canadian whiskies are aged six years (some premiums twelve or more years) and if aged less than four years it must be stated on the label. There is little government intervention as to distiller's formulas, barrel aging, or distilling proofs (all of which are guarded as trade secrets) as it is assumed the distiller will know better what the consumer wants than the government. More expensive Canadian whiskies will generally have a greater concentration of straight whiskies, longer aging, and fewer flavorings as well as being bottled in Canada (cheaper Canadian whisky is shipped in barrels at barrel strength to be reduced and bottled in the country of destination).

VODKA

Vodka originated in Russia and Poland in the 16th century where multiple pot still distillations were used to produce a high strength spirit suitable for transport in the cold climate without freezing. Today it is produced in many countries including Russia, Poland, Sweden, Finland, Holland, and the United States. Vodka is usually unaged with better examples being produced from grains (potatoes, beets and molasses may also be used, with molasses favored for mass produced generic varieties). It is often distilled at high strength in continuous stills with the additional step of charcoal filtering to produce a nearly neutral product although better vodkas fermented from grains are distilled in pot stills (often more than once) to bring out complex flavors and fragrances. Vodkas may also be flavored during the final distillation with fruits, berries, spices, grasses, and herbs, with new producers and varieties appearing periodically. Vodka's current success as a mixer with juice, tonic, soda, etc., is said to have originated with a Hollywood restaurateur in the late 1940's. Having a large overstock of ginger beer and no hope for selling it as it was, he began mixing it with other products without luck until he tried vodka. The cocktail, a "Moscow Mule," caught on and opened the door to vodka's future popularity as a mixer.

GIN

Gin was created in the 17th century by the Dutch doctor Franciscus de la Boe for use as a diuretic (the medicinal effect of juniper berries). He named it Genièver (French for juniper), which came to be known as "Genever" by the Dutch, and later as "Gin" by the English. It was discovered by 17th century English soldiers who referred to it as "Dutch Courage," and by the 18th century, it had become the national drink of England (in large part because it was so inexpensive and readily available). Today, Gin is produced in many countries around the world including Holland, England, Belgium, Norway, Spain, the United States, Germany, and Israel.

Fundamentally, gin is an alcoholic beverage produced from grains and flavored with juniper berries and other botanicals (lemon and orange peels, coriander, angelica, ginger, cardamom, orris root, cassia, licorice, anise, etc.), the recipes for which are kept a secret by the various producers. There are two different styles of gin both of which are rarely aged: Dutch gin and English or American gin (sometimes referred to as dry gin, although the term is misleading as both styles of gin are similarly dry).

Dutch Gin is produced from grains and distilled in pot stills (often with multiple distillations) at a lower distillate strength so as to allow more flavors and aromas to be present in the final spirit. Juniper berries and other flavoring are added to the final distillation to give the gin its characteristic flavor. Dutch gins tend to be fuller, richer gins, that are more commonly consumed without the addition of mixers.

English or American Gin is also produced from grains (mostly corn) but is distilled in continuous stills at a high proof to render a nearly neutral spirit. This spirit is then redistilled, often in pot stills, with juniper berries and other botanicals to create its specific gin style. In general, English or American Gin is more flavored than Dutch gins with a lighter, crisper base more suitable for mixing.

Less expensive gin, called **Compound Gin**, may also be produced from neutral spirits but instead of redistilling the spirit with the many botanicals, it is simply mixed with the essences of juniper and other various flavorings.

RUM

Rum production began in the Caribbean Islands as a by-product of the sugar industry. In 1493 Columbus made a return voyage to the West Indies bringing with him sugarcane cuttings from the Canary Islands. The plant flourished, and in a short time had spread all over the Caribbean. When sugarcane is processed, the cane is crushed to remove the juice which is then heated to crystallize the sugar into large chunks. The remaining liquid, or molasses, was of no value to the sugar producers of the time, and was simply left out as waste. It was noticed that this sweet sticky syrup was fermenting in the hot sun, and by the middle of the 17th century, distillation had become widespread, giving the rum industry its start. Today rum is produced all over the world, almost always near those areas which grow and process sugarcane.

Rum is an alcoholic beverage produced from any of the various sugarcane by-products, distilled at no more than 190 proof, and bottled at no less than 80 proof (with some bottled at 151 proof). Nearly all rums are blended spirits which may sometimes be spiced, and are labeled in one of three ways:

White or Silver Rums having little character as they are usually distilled at high strength in continuous stills and charcoal filtered to minimize flavors and aromas,

Gold or Amber Rums having more flavor due to lower distillation strengths and oak aging, and

Dark Rums being the richest and fullest of rums which are usually distilled in pot stills and aged for longer periods in oak (although the darker color is often from the addition of caramel coloring).

Each of the rum producing islands in the Caribbean (as well as other areas) have its own unique style of rum, although the United States government does not recognize particular styles, but instead the rum's area of origin. Some of the more popular Caribbean Island rums are:

Jamaican Rum: Fuller, richer rums fermented from molasses with a small amount of "dunder" or skimmings from a previous distillation added to the mash in the style of "sour mash" whiskey production. This mash is then allowed to ferment naturally from the action of wild yeast. Jamaican rum is usually double distilled in pot stills at lower distillation strengths and aged in oak casks for years, often five or more.

Puerto Rican Rum: Light and medium body rums fermented in the "sour mash" style and usually distilled in continuous stills at no less than 160 proof, and aged for at least one year (three years or more for gold or amber varieties) in charred or uncharred oak barrels.

The Virgins Islands, Trinidad, and ***Cuba*** produce light style rums in continuous stills while ***Barbados*** produces sweet golden rums in both pot and continuous stills. ***Haiti*** and ***Martinique*** produce heavier rums from sugarcane juice rather than molasses, and distill in pot stills in the French brandy-producing style.

TEQUILA

The Aztecs, in the third century B.C., were the first to produce a fermented beverage from the mezcal plant, a milky, slightly sour, nutritious drink called pulque. The Spaniards brought distillation to Mexico in the 16th century and local mezcal production began. Fundamentally, mezcal is a spirit produced anywhere in Mexico from any of the hundreds of varieties of the mezcal plant (which is not a cactus but rather a member of the amaryllis family). Tequila indi-

> *The infamous worm found in a bottle of mezcal (an agave grub) may have been the local method for "proofing" the spirit. If the worm disintegrated the spirit was underproof, and if it remained intact the spirit was of proper strength.*

cates a mezcal produced from the blue agave plant (the best of the many varieties of mezcal) in the delimited area surrounding the town of Tequila in Jalisco, Mexico. This particular area got its name from the volcanic ash soil and the many dead volcanic cones which break up the otherwise flat landscape (*tel* refers to hill, and *quilla* refers to a type of lava).

Tequila production begins with the blue agave plant which reaches maturity in ten to twelve years, producing a pineapple like base, called a pina, which can weigh as much as 150 pounds. This base is cooked to release a sugar-rich liquid which is fermented, often with wild yeasts, to produce pulque (because of the time it takes the mezcal plant to mature, the Mexican government allows for up to 49% other fermentable substances to be added to the must while still allowing the spirit to retain the name tequila, although high quality tequilas are produced from 100% blue agave). The pulque is then distilled, with better tequilas being double distilled in pot stills.

Tequila is regulated by the government, although enforcement can be lax so be wary of label claims by less reputable producers (particularly as to the percentage of blue agave used in production). Currently the better tequila producers are putting pressure on the government to remedy this situation.

Silver Tequila is the basic spirit, clear in color, and unaged.

Gold Tequila may be aged in oak although it has no legal definition, and often receives caramel coloring to achieve its characteristic color.

Reposado Tequila "rests" in oak for several months, and

Anejo Tequila guarantees at least one year aging in oak, with some better tequilas receiving three years or more.

BRANDY

Brandy is a spirit distilled from fermented fruit (most often grapes) which is usually aged in wood, sometimes up to sixty years. It is produced in countries all over the world including France, the United States, Italy, Mexico, Germany, Spain, South Africa, and Australia. Although the process of distillation had been known for centuries, brandy did not develop until the sixteenth century. At that time, the countries of France and Holland engaged in trade, notably in salt and wine. It is said that a particularly smart and thrifty Dutch shipper came upon the idea of removing the water from the wine he carried (through distillation) so as to increase cargo space on his small boat. Upon his arrival in Holland he planned to replace the water, but his friends preferred the new drink, which eventually became known as *Brandewijn* or "burned wine" in reference to the process of distillation.

COGNAC: Considered to be the finest of all brandy, it refers to brandy produced in the designated A.O.C. region surrounding the city of Cognac on the Charente River, and includes six ranked vineyard areas or "crus:"

Grand Champagne in the very heart of the district, where the city of Cognac is located,

Petite Champagne immediately surrounding Grand Champagne,

Borderies, the smallest of the six located northwest of Cognac and, continuing outward,

Fins Bois,

Bons Bois and

Bois Ordinaires.

Cognac is produced from white grapes only (primarily Ugni Blanc, with Folle Blanche, Colombard, and up to 10% other white grapes), selected for their high yields and their high acid/low alcohol outputs which render a thin, bitter wine ideal for Cognac production. The grapes are fermented with their skins and seeds and double-distilled in traditional pot stills as no continuous stills are permitted in the Cognac region. The distillation process for Cognac is an involved one, demanding the skill and knowledge of many people, and is carried out by either the individual farmer or by regional distillers, both of which are carefully supervised by the government. It is in the unique distillation process, as well as the climate and the chalky soil (most prevalent around the city of Cognac) which is responsible for the high quality of fine Cognacs. After distillation, the brandy is sold to shippers for aging, blending and bottling. Cognac is aged in casks of oak usually from the Limousin or Troncais Forests, with the spirit transferred to used casks after the first year as new oak is too tannic for extended aging. The Cognac will continue to improve in the barrel for up to sixty years as it interacts with the wood and air, slowly evaporating and becoming less alcoholic and more mellow (the ideal age for high quality Cognacs is between twenty-five and forty years). Following aging the Cognac is blended with other Cognacs in large oak vats, and distilled water or diluted brandy is added to reduce the spirit to shipping strength (40 to 43% alcohol). Caramel coloring may also be added to insure a consistent color. Once bottled Cognac will neither improve nor deteriorate until opened, at which time air will gradually oxidize the spirit.

No age statements are permitted on Cognac shipped to the United States, although by law it must be aged at least two and a half years. Most cognacs are bottled with a ***Proprietary Name*** (*Rémy Martin, Courvoisier*, etc.) and/or by ***Area Of Origin*** (*Grande Champagne, Petite Champagne*, etc.). A star system may also be used, with one to five stars generally indicating increasing quality, with three stars guaranteeing that the Cognac was aged at least two and a half years in wood. A letter system was also developed to identify quality Cognacs which is based upon the English language as the English export market has always been important:

C = Cognac,
E = Extra or Especial,
F = Fine,
O = Old,
P = Pale,

S = Superior,
V = Very, and
X = Extra.

The terms **VO** (Very Old), **VSOP** (Very Special Old Pale), and **Reserve** indicate a Cognac with a minimum of four and a half years aging in wood. **Extra** and **Napoléon** Cognacs are aged a minimum of six and a half years in wood, and the term **"Fine Champagne"** indicates a Cognac produced from grapes grown in the Grand or Petite Champagne districts with at least 50% coming from Grand Champagne ("Fine" without the addition of the term "Champagne" may indicate only a French brandy and not necessarily a Cognac).

> *"The great thing about making Cognac is that it teaches you above everything else to wait - man proposes, but time and God and the seasons have got to be on your side."*
> Jean Monnet

ARMAGNAC: Located southeast of Bordeaux in Gascony, Armagnac was divided into three smaller A.O.C. areas in 1936:

Bas Armagnac to the west (where the soil is the sandiest, producing the finest Armagnac),
Tenareze, and
Haut-Armagnac.

The appellation ***Armagnac*** indicates a blend of brandy from any of the three delimited areas, while a specific appellation indicates a blend (or occasionally unblended Armagnac) from that named area. Armagnac is produced from white grapes only with the Ugni Blanc being the most prevalent grape, and is distilled in a form of continuous still which allows for a lower distillate strength, producing a rounder, more flavorful brandy (the traditional Cognac pot still is also used so as to provide more blending options). Traditionally Armagnac has been aged in barrels of black oak from Monlezun but its scarcity is making oak from Limousin and Troncais more common. Armagnac is labeled as to quality in a similar manner as Cognac (VS, VSOP, etc.) with many Armagnac being aged ten years, and is bottled between 40 and 43% alcohol.

CALIFORNIA BRANDY: A spirit produced from 100% California grapes grown mostly in the San Joachin Valley, its major grapes include the Thompson Seedless, Emperor, and the Flame Tokay, although some producers are using the more common French grape varieties to produce a California "Cognac." The continuous still is commonly used because of its uniformity of production and because of its ability to produce a "clean" spirit (while also retaining many important flavorings). The pot still is also used to provide additional blending alternatives and to create particular styles. California brandies are aged in American white oak, often from previous whiskey uses, and must be aged at least two years in wood (with some aged twelve years or more) and be bottled at no less than 40% alcohol.

MEXICAN BRANDY: Mexico didn't begin making Brandy in earnest until the 1950's but today it is the most popular spirit in the country, outselling both tequila and rum. It is home to the world's biggest selling brand, Presidente, the production of which is in excess of five million cases annually. Grapes used in Mexican brandy production include the Thompson seedless, Flame Tokay, Palomino, and St. Émilion (Ugni Blanc). Distillation occurs in both pot and continuous stills, and some Mexican brandy utilizes the Spanish solera system for aging.

POMACE BRANDY: A spirit produced from the skins, seeds, and stalks left behind after the initial pressing of the grapes, it is often bottled directly and consumed young, although some varieties may be aged in oak. The French refer to their pomace brandy as *Marc* (often produced in Burgundy), While the Italians call their's *Grappa.* No specific legal regions exist for Italian Grappa, and they are labeled by either proprietary names or by their grape variety. California also makes a pomace brandy, borrowing the Italian name Grappa. Pomace brandy is usually clear in color and often harsh to drink, and is considered an acquired taste.

FRUIT BRANDY: A spirit produced from the fermented mash of fruits other than grapes, with its most popular varieties being pear brandy (eau-de-vie de poire) and apple brandy. *Calvados* is a French apple brandy having its own appellation, with the finest being *Pays d' Auge*, a Calvados which is double distilled in pot stills and aged for up to forty years. *Applejack*, a United States apple brandy, is also double distilled in pot stills and aged for a minimum of two years but often much longer. Fruit brandies produced from stone fruits include *Kirsch* and *Kirschwasser* (Cherry Brandy), *Mirabelle* (Plum Brandy), and *Barack Palinka* (Apricot Brandy from Hungary). Berry fruit brandies include

Framboise (Raspberry Brandy), ***Fraise*** (Strawberry Brandy), and Blackberry Brandy. Fruit brandies (with no flavorings or sugars added) are generally expensive as a large quantity of fruit is required for production. They are colorless when they receive no aging, and they are usually bottled at their distillation strength of around 100 proof. Countries which produce fruit brandy include the United States, Switzerland, France, Hungary and Germany.

LIQUEURS

Liqueurs (known also as cordials) originated in the middle ages with alchemists, who were interested in creating both spiritually and physically healing mixtures. Apothecaries of the 16th and 17th centuries continued the work, searching for proper combinations of herbs, spices, flowers, etc. to heal specific aliments. By the 18th century, Europe was gathering sugar, spices and fruits from around the world, and liqueur production became less medicinally oriented, and more taste oriented. Liqueurs with names like *Illicit Love, Rose without Thorns*, and *Liqueur des Belles* illustrated the new style and illustrated also the growing interest of women to these new styles. Today, there is a large selection of liqueurs available, some with recipes dating back almost 500 years, while others have a more recent history.

Fundamentally a liqueur is a beverage created by mixing a spirit or spirits (often neutral spirits, brandy, or whiskey) with certain flavoring agents (fruits, herbs, spices, roots, peels, etc. - sometimes with more than 100 different flavors in a single liqueur) to create a new and unique alcoholic beverage. Sweeteners from a variety of sources are also added, sometimes comprising as much as 35% of the finished product, and colorings may be added to brighten the blend and guarantee a uniform appearance.

There are two basic ways to extract aromas and flavors from a flavoring agent: Maceration and distillation. **Maceration** involves the soaking of a flavoring agent(s) in alcohol until the alcohol has sufficiently absorbed its essence (when a flavoring agent is soaked in water it is instead called infusion). This process can last as long as a year, and is generally used with those agents which may be sensitive to heat such as softer fruits. A related technique is percolation or "brewing," a process involving pumping alcohol or water through the flavoring agent (for weeks or months) until the essence has been obtained. ***Distillation*** is used with those flavoring agents not sensitive to heat (seeds, herbs, peels, etc.). The flavorings are steeped in alcohol for a few hours, then distilled with the spirit in a pot still, often more than once.

Some of the more famous liqueurs include:

*****Bénédictine D.O.M.***, a Cognac based liqueur, is the most famous of French liqueurs. The label initials D.O.M. stand for *Deo Optimo Maximo* - "To God, Most Good, Most Great." Originated by the Bénédictine monk Dom Bernardo Vincelli in 1510, the original recipe (involving twenty-seven different herbs and plants) was lost for hundreds of years until 1863 when it was rediscovered in forgotten manuscripts. The company is now owned by a private family who closely guard the recipe (only three individuals at any given time know the full details). It is truly a unique product, involving five individual macerations or distillations with each receiving separate oak barrel aging. At any given time there are more than 30,000 barrels of incomplete and complete Bénédictine maturing in the cellars of the distillery. It has never been successfully copied, although hundreds of producers have tried. In the 1930's, noting a trend to drier liqueurs, B&B (Bénédictine and Brandy) was introduced, a mixture of 60% liqueur with 40% additional Cognac.

Chartreuse: Produced by French Carthusian Monks, Chartreuse is a 110 proof brandy-based herbal liqueur originated in 1605. The recipe was finalized in 1764, calling for the use of 130 different plants. In 1838 yellow Chartreuse (80 proof) was introduced, being somewhat sweeter and less aromatic than the original green Chartreuse.

Cointreau: One of the finest orange liqueurs, it employs the peels of bitter oranges from Haiti and Curacao, in addition to peels from Mediterranean sweet oranges added to a neutral spirit base. It is a lighter, less complex orange liqueur with a clean aftertaste.

Grand Marnier: Although classified as an orange liqueur, it is produced with a Cognac base instead of the more common neutral spirit base. It is produced from the peels of bitter oranges (no Mediterranean oranges are used), and aged in large oak casks for a year and a half. It is a more complex orange liqueur with definite Cognac undertones.

Drambuie: A whisky based liqueur produced in Scotland from mostly Highland malt whiskies and secret herb flavorings, and aged from eight to twenty years. It takes its name from the Gaelic An dram buidheach, "the drink that satisfies."

Bailey's Irish Cream: A newcomer to the world of liqueurs, Bailey's was introduced in the 1970's and quickly seized almost a quarter of the entire liqueur market. It is a mixture of Irish Whiskey and dairy cream, carefully produced to inhibit the cream's curdling and to insure a reasonable shelf life.

Amaretto Di Saronno: Produced in Italy from apricot pits (which have a strong almond flavor) and various herbs in a neutral spirit base, it is the original "amaretto liqueur."

Kahlúa and ***Tia Maria*** are coffee based liqueurs, the former from Mexico, the latter produced in Jamaica from local Blue Mountain coffee with a rum base.

Some of the more common generic liqueurs include: *Amaretto* (apricot stones), *Anisette* (aniseed), *Crème de Cacao* (cacao seeds and vanilla beans), *Crème de Cassis* (black currants), *Crème de Menthe* (a variety of mints, mostly peppermint), *Crème de Noyaux* (fruit stones), *Curacao* (peels of bitter oranges from the Island of Curacao), *Sambuca* (elderbush berries), and *Sloe Gin* (sloe berries).

> *Créme indicates a liqueur produced from a specific flavoring agent, while cream indicates dairy cream as that used in Bailey's Irish Cream.*

INDEX

Acid In Wine, Defined 12
Ahr (Germany) 69
Alcohol, Defined 9
Ale 91
Alexander Valley (Sonoma County) 56
Almeda County (California) 57
Aloxe-Corton (Côte de Beaune) 42
Alsace (France) 31 - 33
Alsace, Appellations Defined 32
Amaretto 128
Amaretto di Saronno 128
Amarone (Italy) 65
Amber Rum 112
American Gin 110
American Viticultural Areas (California) 53
American Whiskey 104 - 106
Amontillado Sherry 82
Anderson Valley (Mendocino County) 57
Anejo Tequila 116

Anisette 128
Anjou (Loire Valley) 25
Appellation d'Origine Contrôlée (A.O.C.) 22
Applejack Brandy 123
Apricot Brandy 123
Armagnac 120 - 121
Auslese (Germany) 72
Australian Wines 75 - 77
Auxey-Duresses (Côte de Beaune) 42

B&B 127
Baden (Germany) 69
Bailey's Irish Cream 128
Barack Palinka 123
Barbados Rum 113
Barbaresco (Italy) 64
Bardolino (Italy) 65
Barleywine 93
Barolo (Italy) 64
Bas Armagnac 121
Beaujolais (France) 45 - 46
Beaujolais Cru 46
Beaujolais Noveau 45
Beaujolais Supérieur 45
Beaujolais-Villages 45
Beaume de Venise (Rhône Valley) 48
Beaune (Cote de Beaune) 42

INDEX

Beer 87 - 94
Beerenauslese (Germany) 72
Bénédictine D.O.M. 126
Bitter (Ale) 91
Blackberry Brandy 124
Blanc de Blancs (Champagne Labeling Term) 30
Blanc de Noirs (Champagne Labeling Term) 30
Blanchots (Chablis) 43
Blended Scotch Whisky 102
Blended Whiskey (U.S.) 106
Bock Beer 91
Bois Ordinaires (Cognac) 117
Bolgheri Russo (Italy) 62
Bonnezeaux (Loire Valley) 25
Bons Bois (Cognac) 117
Bordeaux (France) 33 - 39
Borderies (Cognac) 117
Botrytis Cinerea (Noble Rot) 17, 38, 65, 72
Bottled In Bond 106
Bougros (Chablis) 43
Bourbon Whiskey 105
Bourgogne (Burgundy), Appellation Defined 41
Bourgogne Aligoté de Bouzeron (Côte Chalonnaise) 44
Bourgueil (Loire Valley) 25
Brandy 116 - 124
Brewing Process (Beer) 89 - 91

Brochon (Côte de Nuit) 42
Brouilly (Beaujolais) 46
Brown Ale 91
Brunello Di Montalcino (Italy) 63
Brut (Champagne Labeling Term) 29
Burgundy (France) 39 - 46

Cabernet Franc (Grape) 18
Cabernet Sauvignon (Grape) 17
California Brandy 121
California Wines 49 - 58
Calvados 123
Cambeltown (Scotland) 100
Cambeltown Single Malts 101
Canadian Whisky 107
Carneros (Napa Valley) 56
Carneros (Sonoma County) 56
Chablis (France) 43
Chablis Appellations, Defined 43
Chambolle-Musigny (Côte de Nuit) 41
Champagne (France) 26 - 30
Chaptalization 60, 68
Chardonnay Grape 16
Chartreuse 127
Chassagne-Montrachet (Côte de Beaune) 42
Château Carbonnieux (Graves) 37
Château, Defined 34

INDEX

Château D'Yquem (Sauternes) 38
Château Grillet (Rhône Valley) 47
Château Haut-Brion (Graves) 35
Château Lafite-Rothschild, (Médoc) 35
Château Latour (Médoc) 35
Château Margaux (Médoc) 35
Château Mouton-Rothschild (Médoc) 35
Château Olivier (Graves) 37
Château Pétrus (Pomerol) 37
Châteauneuf-du-Pape (Rhône Valley) 48
Cheilly-Les-Maranges (Côte de Beaune) 42
Chénas (Beaujolais) 46
Chenin Blanc Grape 17
Cherry Brandy 123
Chianti (Tuscany) 62
Chinon (Loire Valley) 25
Chiroubles (Beaujolais) 46
Chorey-Les-Beaune (Côte de Beaune) 42
Claret, Defined 34
Classified Châteaus 37
Clos, Defined 34
Cognac 117 - 120
Cointreau 127
Colheita Port 85
Comblanchien (Côte de Nuit) 42
Compound Gin 111
Condrieu 47

Continuous Still, Defined 96
Corgoloin (Côte de Nuit) 42
Corn Whiskey 105
Cornas (Rhône Valley) 48
Côte Châlonnaise (France) 43
Côte de Beaune 42
Côte de Beaune-Villages 41
Côte de Brouilly (Beaujolais) 46
Côte de Nuit 41 - 42
Côte de Nuit-Villages 41
Côte d'Or 41 - 42
Côte du Rhône (Rhône Valley) 47
Côte Rôtie (Rhône Valley) 47
Coteaux Champenois (Champagne Labeling Term) 30
Coteaux Du Layon (Loire Valley) 25
Côtes de Blaye (Bordeaux) 34
Côtes de Bourg (Bordeaux) 34
Côtes du Rhône-Villages (Rhône Valley) 47
Côtes du Ventoux (Rhône Valley) 48
Cream Sherry 82
Crémant (Champagne Labeling Term) 30
Crémant d' Alsace 32
Crémant de Loire 25
Crème de Cacao 128
Crème de Cassis 128
Crème de Menthe 128

Crème de Noyaux 129
Crozes-Hermitage (Rhône Valley) 47
Crus Bourgeois Of Médoc, Defined 35
Cuban Rum 113
Curacao 129
Cuvée, Defined 26
Cuvée de Prestige (Champagne Labeling Term) 30

Dark Rum 112
Decanting 13
Dégorgement (Méthode Champenoise) 29
Demi-Sec (Champagne Labeling Term) 29
Denominazione di Origine Controllata (D.O.C.), Italy 60
Denominazione di Origine Controllata E Garantita (D.O.C.G.), Italy 61
Deuxièmes Cru (Sauternes) 38
Dezize-Les-Maranges (Côte de Beaune) 42
Distillation 96
Distillation (In Liqueur Production) 126
Domaine, Defined 34
Dominus 54
Doublebock Beer 91
Doux (Champagne Labeling Term) 29
Drambuie 128
Dry Creek Valley (Sonoma County) 56

Dutch Gin 110

Edna Valley (San Luis Obispo) 58
Eiswein (Germany) 72
English Gin 110
Entre-deux-Mers (Bordeaux) 34
Estate Bottled (Burgundy) 39
Estate Bottled (California) 53
Extra (Cognac) 120
Extra Dry (Champagne Labeling Term) 29

Fermentation, Defined 10
Fine Champagne (Cognac) 120
Fino Sherry 81
Fins Bois (Cognac) 117
Fixin (Côte de Nuit) 41
Flagey- Echézeaux (Côte de Nuit) 41
Fleurie (Beaujolais) 46
Flor (Sherry) 81
Fortified Wine, Defined 11
Fraise 124
Framboise 124
Franken (Germany) 69
French Pronunciation, Rules 24
French Wine 21 - 48
   Alsace 31 - 33
   Bordeaux 33 - 39

INDEX

   Burgundy 39 - 46
   Champagne 26 - 30
   French Wine in General 21 - 24
   French Wine, Map 23
   Loire Valley 24 - 26
   Rhône Valley 46 - 48
Fruit Brandy 123

Gamay Grape 18
Geographic Location, Importance of to Wine 14
German Wines 67 - 73
Gevrey-Chambertin (Côte de Nuit) 41
Gewürztraminer Grape 17
Gewürztraminer Wine (Alsace) 31
Gigondas (Rhône Valley) 48
Gin 109 - 111
Givry (Côte Châlonnaise) 43
Gold Rum 112
Gold Tequila 116
Grains, In Beer 88
Grand Champagne (Cognac) 117
Grand Cru Wine (Burgundy), Appellation 41
Grand Crus Bourgeois Exceptionnels of Médoc,
     Defined 35
Grand Crus Bourgeois of Médoc, Defined 35
Grand Crus Classés (Bordeaux) 35
Grand Marnier 127

Grand Premiere Cru (Sauternes) 38
Grape Varieties 16 - 19
Grappa 123
Graves (Bordeaux) 37 - 39
Graves, Appellations Defined 37
Grenache Grape 18
Grenouilles (Chablis) 43
Guenoc Valley (Lake County) 57

Haitian Rum 113
Haut-Armagnac 121
Haut-Médoc 36
Hermitage (Rhône Valley) 47
Hessische Bergstrasse (Germany) 69
Highland Single Malt Whiskies 101
Highlands (Scotland) 100
Hops (in Beer) 88
Howell Mountain (Napa Valley) 55

Insignia 54
Institut National des Appellations d'Origine des Vins Et Eaux-de-Vie 21
Ireland 103
Irish Whiskey 103
Islay (Scotland) 100
Islay Single Malts 101
Italian Wines 59 - 65

INDEX

Jamaican Rum 113
Juliénas (Beaujolais) 46
Jura (Scotland) 100

Kabinett (Germany) 71
Kahlúa 128
Kirsch 123
Kirschwasser 123
Krausening 90

La Coulée de Serrant (Loire Valley) 25
La Roche Aux Moines (Loire Valley) 25
La Tâche (Côte de Nuit) 41
Ladoix-Serrigny (Côte de Beaune) 42
Lager 91
Lake County (California) 57
Lambic 93
Landwein (Germany) 71
Late Bottled Vintage Port 84
Les Clos (Chablis) 43
Les Preuses (Chablis) 43
Liqueur de Tirage (Champagne) 28
Liqueurs 124 - 129
Lirac (Rhône Valley) 48
Listrac (Médoc) 36
Livermore Valley (Almeda County) 58

Loire Valley (France) 24 - 26
Lowlands (Scotland) 100
Lowland Single Malts 101

Maceration, in Liqueurs 125
Mâconnais (France) 44 - 45
Mâcon Blanc 44
Mâcon Supérieur 44
Mâcon-Villages 44
Manzanilla Sherry 82
Marc (Brandy) 123
Margaux (Médoc) 36
Marlstone 54
Marsannay-la-Côte (Côte de Nuit) 41
Martinique Rum 113
McDowell Valley (Mendocino County) 57
Médoc (Bordeaux) 34 - 36
Mendocino County (California) 56
Mercurey (Côte Châlonnaise) 43
Meritage (California) 54
Merlot Grape 18
Méthode Champenoise 27
Meursault (Côte de Beaune) 42
Mexican Brandy 122
Mezcal 114
Mild (Ale) 91
Mirabelle 123

INDEX

Mittelrhein (Germany) 69
Modesto (California) 58
Montagny (Côte Châlonnaise) 43
Monterey County (California) 57
Monthélie (Côte de Beaune) 42
Morey St-Denis (Côte de Nuit) 41
Morgon (Beaujolais) 46
Mosel-Saar-Ruwer (Germany) 69
Moulin-à-Vent (Beaujolais) 46
Moulis (Médoc) 36
Mount Veeder (Napa Valley) 56
Mull (Scotland) 100
Muscadet (Loire Valley) 25

Nahe (Germany) 69
Napa Valley (California) 55
Napoléon (Cognac) 120
Nebbiolo Grape 19
Neutral Spirits, Defined 97
New South Wales (Australia) 76
Noble Rot 17, 38, 65, 72
Non-Vintage (Champagne Labeling Term) 30
Nuits St-Georges (Côte de Nuit) 41

Oakville (Napa Valley) 55
Old Ale 92
Oloroso Sherry 82

Opus One 54
Orkney Islands (Scotland) 100

Pale Ale 91
Pauillac (Médoc) 36
Pays D' Auge (Calvados) 123
Pear Brandy (Eau-de-Vie de Poire) 123
Pedro Ximénex Sherry 82
Percolation, in Liqueurs 126
Pernand-Vergelesses (Côte de Beaune) 42
Pessac-Léognan (Graves) 38
Petit Chablis 43
Petite Champagne (Cognac) 117
Pfalz (Germany) 69
Phylloxera 15, 98
Piedmont (Italy) 63
Pilsner 91
Pilsner Urquell 91
Pinot Blanc Wines (Alsace) 31
Pinot Grigio (Italy) 65
Pinot Noir Grape 17
Plum Brandy 123
Pomace Brandy 122
Pomerol (Bordeaux) 37
Pommard (Côte de Beaune) 42
Port 83 - 86
Porter 93

INDEX

Pot Still, Defined 96
Pouilly Fumé (Loire Valley) 25
Pouilly Sur Loire (Loire Valley) 25
Pouilly-Fuissé (Mâconnais) 45
Pouilly-Vinzelles (Mâconnais) 44
Prädikat Wines (Germany) 71
Premier Cru (Burgundy), Appellation Defined 41
Premier Cru (Sauternes) 38
Premières Côtes de Bordeaux 34
Prissey (Côte de Nuit) 42
Proof, Defined 97
Proprietary Wines (California) 52
Proprietor Grown (California) 54
Puerto Rican Rum 113
Puligny-Montrachet (Côte de Beaune) 42
Pulque 114

Qualitätswein Bestimmter Anbaugebiete (Q.b.A.) 71
Qualitätswein Mit Prädikat (Prädikat Or Q.m.P.) 71
Quarts de Chaume (Loire Valley) 25

Raspberry Brandy 124
Rasteau (Rhône Valley) 48
Recioto Della Valpolicella-Amarone (Italy) 65
Regional Wines, Defined In Bordeaux 33

Régnié (Beaujolais) 46
Reisling Grape 16
Reisling Wine (Alsace) 31
Remuage (Méthode Champenoise) 28
Reposado Tequila 116
Reserve (California) 54
Reserve (Cognac) 120
Rheingau (Germany) 69
Rheinhessen (Germany) 69
Rhône Valley (France) 46 - 48
Riddling (Méthode Champenoise) 28
Romanée-Conti (Côte de Nuit) 41
Rosé (Champagne Labeling Term) 30
Ruby Port 84
Rully (Côte Châlonnaise) 43
Rum 111 - 113
Russian River Valley (Sonoma County) 56
Rutherford (Napa Valley) 55
Rye Whiskey 105

Saale-Unstrut (Germany) 69
Sachsen (Germany) 69
Sambuca 129
Sampigny-Les- Maranges (Côte de Beaune) 42
San Joaquin Valley (California) 58
San Luis Obispo (California) 58
Sancerre (Loire Valley) 25

INDEX

Sangiovese Grape 18
Santa Barbara County (California) 58
Santa Clara County (California) 57
Santa Maria Valley (Santa Barbara County) 58
Santa Ynez Valley (Santa Barbara County) 58
Santenay (Côte de Beaune) 42
Sassicaia (Italy) 61
Saumur (Loire Valley) 25
Sauternes (Bordeaux) 38
Sauvignon Blanc Grape 17
Savennières (Loire Valley) 25
Savigny-Les-Beaune (Côte de Beaune) 42
Scotland 99
Scottish Ale 92
Sec (Champagne Labeling Term) 29
Sémillon Grape 17
Sherry 79 - 83
Silver Rum 112
Silver Tequila 116
Single Malt Whisky 100
Single Quinta Port 85
Skye (Scotland) 100
Sloe Gin 129
Soave (Italy) 65
Soil, Importance of to Wine 14
Solera System (Sherry) 80
Sonoma County (California) 56

Sour Mash Whiskey 105
South Australia 76
Sparkling Wine, Defined 11
Spätlese (Germany) 72
Speyside (Scotland) 100
Spirits in General 95
St-Joseph (Rhône Valley) 47
St-Romain (Côte de Beaune) 42
St. Estèphe (Médoc) 36
St. Julien (Médoc) 36
Stags Leap District (Napa Valley) 56
St-Amour (Beaujolais) 46
St-Aubin (Côte de Beaune) 42
Steam Beer 92
St-Émilion (Bordeaux) 37
Stout 93
St-Péray (Rhône Valley) 48
Straight Whiskey (U.S.) 105
Strawberry Brandy 124
St-Véran (Mâconnais) 44
Sur Lie, Defined 26
Süss-Reserve (Germany) 68
Sweet Mash Whiskey 105
Syrah Grape 18

Table Wine, Defined 11
Tafelwein (Germany) 70

INDEX

Tannin In Wine, Defined 12
Tavel (Rhone Valley) 48
Tawny Port 84
Tenareze (Armagnac) 121
Tennessee Whiskey 106
Tequila 114 - 116
Tia Maria 128
Tokay Pinot Gris (Alsace) 31
Trappist Beer 93
Trinidad Rum 113
Trockenbeerenauslese (Germany) 72
Tuscany (Italy) 62

United States Whiskey 104 - 106

Valmur (Chablis) 43
Valpolicella (Italy) 65
Varietal Wines (California) 52
Vatted Malt Whisky (Scotland) 102
Vaudésir (Chablis) 43
Veneto (Italy) 64
Victoria (Australia) 77
Vinification, Defined 19
Vino da Tavola (Italy) 60
Vino Nobile Di Montepulciano (Italy) 63
Vins de Pays 22
Vins de Table 22

Vins Délimités de Qualité Supérieure (V.D.Q.S.) 22
Vintage (Champagne Labeling Term) 30
Vintage Character Port 85
Vintage Date (California) 54
Vintage Port 84
Vintage Release Port 85
Vintner Grown (California) 54
Viognier Grape 17
Virgins Islands Rum 113
Vodka 108 - 109
Volnay (Côte de Beaune) 42
Vosne-Romanée (Côte de Nuit) 41
Vougeot (Côte de Nuit) 41
Vouvray (Loire Valley) 24
VSOP (Cognac) 120
VSOP (Armagnac) 121

Water, In Beer 87
Weather, Importance of to Grapes 15
Weisse Beer 93
Weizenbier 93
Western Australia 77
Western Isles (Scotland) 100
Wheat Beer 93
Wheat Whiskey 106
Whiskey 98 - 107

INDEX

Whiskey Production 98 - 99
White Port 85
White Rum 112
Wine in General 11 - 19
Wood Port 83
Württemberg (Germany) 69

Yeast, In Beer 88

Zinfandel Grape 18

ORDER FORM

Interested in ordering this book or other titles?

TELEPHONE ORDERS: Have your credit card ready and call ***Toll Free: 1-888-44BOOKS***

POSTAL ORDERS: Send check, money order, or credit card information to:

Copacetic Publications
1127 Crescent St.
Sarasota, FL 34242 USA

Please send ____ copies of *Wine, Beer and Spirits*: *The Concise Guide* to:

_____
_____
_____

Credit Card #:_____
Exp._____ Name on Card: _____

Shipping: $1.50 for the first book, and 50 cents for each additional book. Allow 2 weeks for delivery. **Tax:** Please add 7% to orders shipped to Florida addresses.